Cursing in Russian with Lenin: An Introduction to Russian "Mat,"
by Mark R. Pettus, PhD

ISBN 978-1-0880-5675-2

Learn more about this and other titles at:
www.russianthroughpropaganda.com

Cursing in Russian with Lenin

An Introduction to Russian "Mat"

by Mark R. Pettus, Ph.D.

Cursing in Russian with Lenin

Russian "mat" — a remarkably expressive, linguistically fascinating, and utterly hilarious system of obscenity that builds a wide variety of words from a handful of extremely vulgar roots — is never taught in the classroom, but is absolutely essential for anyone looking to master Russian in all of its fullness. Russians widely consider "mat" to be much more obscene than anything in English. Its words were long unprintable, and their use in public performances remains punishable by Russian law. Yet when Russians really want to make their feelings known, many will resort to "mat" — for it alone has the power to express everything from utter despair, to incandescent rage, to bottomless disdain, to uproarious defiance of a fallen world.

This beginner's guide introduces the basics of "mat" in an in-depth yet manageable fashion, including detailed descriptions of word-building principles, the literal and figurative meanings of "mat" expressions, and extensive coverage of euphemism — explaining how Russians can use "mat" without *really* using it! The text presents a manageable list of all the basic "mat" vocabulary — nouns, verbs, adjectives, and phrases — that you'll actually hear, with simple examples of usage. English transliterations are provided alongside the original Russian Cyrillic (marked for stress!), making this book useful both for serious students of Russian and for inquirers who don't even know the alphabet. Along the way, we'll review certain key points of Russian declension, conjugation, and grammar in a refreshingly obscene context.

For anyone with a sense of humor and an appreciation of the "lower" registers of human experience and expression, "mat" is sure to become one of the real joys of learning the Russian language. Embark on this journey of discovery — with Lenin as your guide!

About the Author...

Originally from Franklin, Tennessee, Mark Pettus holds a PhD in Slavic Languages and Literatures from Princeton University. Altogether, he's spent around six years living, studying, and working in Russia. Today he is a lecturer in Slavic Languages and Literatures at Princeton. Mark is the author of the *Russian Through Propaganda* textbook series (Books 1 and 2), and its continuation, *Russian Through Poems and Paintings* (Books 3 and 4). He has also published a growing library of Russian parallel-language readers — the *Reading Russian* series.

Check out **www.russianthroughpropaganda.com** for a variety of resources for students of Russian language, literature, and culture.

Contents

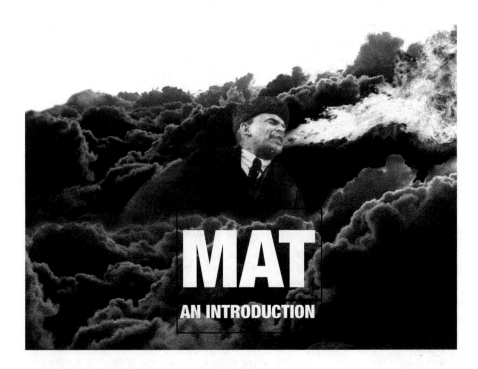

What is this book? (read before buying!)

Before we even begin discussing "mat," we should make clear what the purpose and scope of this book is: to give serious students of Russian (and, to a lesser extent, the merely curious) a solid introduction to the basic expressions, word-building principles, and systematic euphemism of Russian cursing known as "mat."

Therefore, this book — although it does list words and typical phrases — is not a simple phrasebook; nor is it a reference dictionary that presumes to cover the topic exhaustively. Indeed, the vocabulary presented here has been deliberately kept to a certain minimum. It focuses on those bread-and-butter "mat" expressions you'll be hearing over and over again in Russian — and which, with a little experience, you might venture to use yourself on occasion without sounding like you're trying too hard.

As we'll soon see, "mat" is extremely flexible in terms of word formation: it takes basic obscene roots and builds a wide variety of words from them, with widely disparate meanings. This allows for countless expressions (many relatively obscure), and even the occasional neologism. For this reason, a book of this size couldn't hope to document every last word of "mat" — nor would that be particularly useful. What's much more important is to grasp both the meanings of the few ubiquitous stock phrases of "mat" that constitute its core vocabulary, and to understand its basic word-building principles. This will equip you to analyze, understand, and appreciate more outlandish and sophisticated "mat" expressions as you encounter them.

Furthermore, the examples of usage provided here have been kept extremely simple, and few in number — keeping in mind that many "mat" phrases are often used in grammatical isolation (as simple interjections). Of course, "mat" verbs are conjugated, and nouns are declined — and these forms will be presented in detail. But many set expressions rarely if ever change.

Nowadays, anyone who wants either to look up a more obscure "mat" term, or see numerous examples of usage for more basic expressions, can easily consult Google. Searching "images" and surveying "mat"-based memes can be especially amusing.

Finally, your best resource when it comes to "mat" are Russian-speaking friends who can explain what an expression means in context — often right after you've heard them use it. The trick is, first, to know "mat" when you hear it (a simple task: all you need is to know a handful of basic roots), and, second, to understand enough about "mat" word formation to make sense of any explanation, remaining sensitive both to the literal meaning of a word and the senses in which it is typically used.

Music is also a great resource for "mat" — particularly more recent rap or punk music. Pioneering bands in the unapologetic use of "mat" in their lyrics include **Сектор газа** (Sektor Gaza) and, especially, **Лениград** (Leningrad). Of course, countless contemporary acts are now following their trailblazing example.

For all of these reasons, this book attempts to be both thorough in its explanations, and as slim as possible. There are plenty of other books and sites where you can find reams of naughty vocabulary; but, to my knowledge, this is the only resource that really explains how "mat" works. And, in my opinion, knowledge of "mat" is simply essential for any serious student of Russian, regardless of whether you "like" it or plan on using it yourself. For those with a sense of humor, it can be one of the real joys of studying Russian.

What is мат?

The term **мат** (pronounced "maht" — as in, open up and say "ah!") refers to a highly limited number of extremely obscene roots that are combined with standard Russian prefixes and suffixes to build countless words with a wide range of meanings. We might think of **мат** as a kind of shadowy version of standard Russian: the grammar and word-formation principles are exactly the same, but at the heart of every **мат** term lurks an unspeakably vulgar root. In many cases, as we'll see, a **мат** term may have a more or less direct equivalent in standard Russian. The difference is all about the root!

This "shadow language" can be used in a literal sense (which is always, at bottom, sexual), but more often it is used either to "curse" ("Fuck!" "Fuck you!" "Fuck that!"

etc.), or — perhaps more surprisingly — to describe almost anything, from sports to things of a technical nature. In these broader contexts, the use of **мат** can certainly express frustration, but it can also be entirely neutral (technical) in tone. For example, you could explain how to assemble a piece of furniture using **мат**, especially if you don't know the technical terms for equipment or components. Think something along the lines of: "Take that fucking whatchamacallit and give a good fuck to that fucking thing there, then keep fucking it until you've fucked it all the way in."

Which words constitute мат?

Needless to say, there are all kinds of "bad" words in Russian, from sexual vocabulary to insults based on nationality, race, gender, sexual orientation, etc. Meanwhile, there's slang of all sorts, which may register as substandard, distasteful, or crude. This includes, by the way, the criminal jargon or "cant" known as **феня** (fenya), which is an entire topic unto itself (for a humorous introduction, check out the classic 1971 Soviet comedy **Джентльмены удачи**, or *Gentlemen of Fortune*). In short, there's all kinds of language one wouldn't use in formal situations or "polite society."

While some of the terms in this book may overlap with these broader categories of offensive speech, and while "bad words" of every description often accompany **мат**, the focus of this book is "mat" in a strict sense: vocabulary built from the four indisputable **мат** roots: **ёб**- (fuck), **хуй** (cock), **пизд**- (cunt), and **блядь** (bitch). A fifth root, **муд**- (scrotum) is also classified here as **мат**, though this decision is certainly debatable (more on that when the time comes). The literal meaning of all of these roots relates to genitalia or sexual acts, and they are all — if to varying degrees — "productive" in the sense that they can be used to create new words, many of which may have little or no connection to the literal meaning of the root. For example, the root **хуй** yields adjectives meaning both "good" and "bad," as well as verbs meaning "to strike."

Certainly, the power of certain non-**мат** words to offend may equal or even exceed that of **мат**. For example, **сука** (bitch — literally, a female dog, as in English) is essentially synonymous with **блядь** (bitch, in the sense of a woman prone to sexual debauchery). To be sure, **сука** is used constantly with **мат**, and any Russian would consider a "bad word." Yet most would probably hesitate to call it **мат** (some might, but most wouldn't). Another example in this regard is **жопа** (asshole) — again, a very bad word, but probably not **мат**.

One argument against classifying these words as **мат** is that they are highly unproductive in terms of word-building. Indeed, this criterion could be cited in excluding **муд**- (scrotum) from the list; although it does produce a handful of extremely common words, they are neither as numerous or as wide-ranging in meaning as those produced from the four undisputed roots of **мат**.

Therefore, keeping our reservations with regard to **муд**- in mind, this book will define **мат** as all words formed from the following five roots: **ёб**- (fuck), **хуй** (cock), **пизд**- (cunt), **блядь** (bitch), and **муд**- (scrotum)

For good measure, this book will conclude with a basic list of words on the margins of **мат**, including **сука** and **жопа**. It's important to understand that many of the words there that English speakers might assume would be **мат** — "shit," for example — are not.

How can мат vocabulary be substituted for "normal" words?

Many examples await, but let's take one now in order to show how **мат** works, both in terms of how it forms words from vulgar roots, and how the resulting words can often be substituted for everyday words that have no vulgar meaning whatsoever.

The basic Russian verb for "to steal" is **укра́сть** (for these examples, we're using the perfective forms of the verbs). Somewhat more colloquial equivalents include **стащи́ть** and **спере́ть**, where the prefix **с-** suggests "off" or "away" (as in, someone "made off with" my wallet).

Following this model, and using the same prefix, we have the **мат** verb **спи́здить**; the only difference, of course, is that the harmless roots of the first two verbs have been replaced by the mat root **пизд-**, best known in the feminine noun **пизда́** (which consists of the root plus the feminine noun ending **-а**). This noun, like the root it's made from, means "vagina"; a closer English equivalent would be "pussy," or, closer yet, the considerably more vulgar (in American English, at least) "cunt."

If we created an imaginary *literal* English equivalent of the verb **стащи́ть**, it might be "to offdrag," as in:

> **Кошелёк стащи́ли!**   They offdragged my wallet!

Following this model, we can approximate the literal meaning of the new **мат** verb we just created:

> **Кошелёк спи́здили!**   They offcunted my wallet!

Note how the meaning of this new verb has nothing to do with "vagina." But it has allowed us to use a vulgar **мат**-based expression in place of a harmless everyday verb. This is essentially how **мат** works; as we'll see, mat roots can be used to create all manner of words — not only verbs. And any word formed in this way occupies much the same stylistic register as the English "fuck." Entire utterances may thus consist exclusively of **мат** vocabulary. Think: "Fucketty-fuck-fuck-fuck..."

We should hasten to add that while innovation is always possible in theory, **мат** vocabulary is basically limited to pre-existing words; that is, you can't take any verb you like and substitute a **мат** root to create an entirely new word. So, you'll have to learn **мат** vocabulary just as you would ordinary Russian vocabulary.

This book will present this basic vocabulary while explaining how each item was built, and providing any obvious non-**мат** equivalents, if such exist. In some cases, verbs formed with prefixes might swap out prefixes to produce new meanings, but these may be far less commonly used. Here, we'll give only the basics.

How bad is мат?

Like so much regarding language, this is ultimately a subjective matter. But it's safe to make one sweeping generalization: Russians regard **мат** as much worse than anything English has to offer. We've already glimpsed how **мат** can be very hard to translate, since doing so in a literal sense would involve creating compound words (like "offcunting") that English simply doesn't allow for. Often, the best translations we can muster involve strewing the word "fucking" everywhere — not "They offcunted my wallet!" but "They stole my fucking wallet!"

But even here we run up against a simple problem of register: Russians don't consider the English "fucking" to be "as bad as" any expression of **мат**. In this sense, no English translation is adequate.

Speaking very generally, a few factors may help explain this attitude. First, **мат** has long been banished from polite society and, until fairly recently, from the printed page. Its use is therefore associated with the "underground" — the criminal underworld, prisoners (Gulag and otherwise), brawling soccer fans, and other lower-class "undesirables" of all kinds. Even today the public use of mat is legally classified as a form of hooliganism (**хулиганство** — and yes, that is the technical legal term!). On top of this, we have traditionally reticent attitudes towards the "unmentionables" of sex (as we've noted, it's certainly no accident that all **мат** roots refer to genitalia or intercourse — and not, for example, to defecation). Combined, these two factors may give some sense of why Russians regard these words as "bad" in a way most English speakers may struggle to understand.

The banishment of **мат** from the official public sphere — still largely in place today — helps reinforce the idea of its "superiority" to obscenity in other languages, especially English. For example, if **мат** is legally barred from public movie screenings, then official Russian-language voiceovers will replace even the "worst words in English" (like "fuck" and "fucking") with relatively mild, non-**мат** expressions. Thus, "Fuck you!" may become something more along the lines of "**Пошёл к чёрту!**" ("Go to the devil!"), instead of the obvious **мат** equivalent: "**Пошёл на хуй!**" (literally, "Go onto a cock!").

Of course, the near-universal awe toward **мат**'s infernal foulness gives rise to conflicting feelings among Russian speakers. Many disdain it and will balk at even acknowledging its existence; like the things it refers to, it is taboo. Meanwhile, other Russians will gush openly concerning its power and expressivity — the likes of which are known to no other language in the world — and will insist that no one *really* knows Russian without knowing **мат**. Most Russians, perhaps, fall somewhere in between. What all these types have in common is a reverence for the power of **мат**.

Here as elsewhere, one may encounter the fanciful notion that the Russian language — like Russian literature, the Russian soul, etc. — contains mysteries that a foreigner cannot possibly hope to comprehend. This is of course utter nonsense; **мат**, like Russian itself, is a language that, though fraught with subtleties, *can* be learned. But part of learning it is learning to appreciate native speakers' perceptions of it, which retain their own validity regardless of how skewed, or simply incorrect, those perceptions may be. Which brings us to our next topic...

Where did мат come from?

Popular perceptions of **мат** as profoundly "bad" help explain the widespread notion that it was introduced by the Mongols during their cataclysmic invasion of Russia in the 13th century: surely language so foul could only have been introduced into "Holy Russia" from without! Unfortunately for Russian xenophobes, this account has no basis whatsoever in fact (the theory itself apparently originated in the 19th century and was then enshrined under the Soviets with support from the writer Maxim Gorky).

In any event, you should be prepared for this little theory to be trotted out whenever your average Russian begins telling you about **мат** — often followed by a litany of plausibly-enough-sounding folk etymologies — for example, that the word **хуй** derives from the Mongol word for "sheath" (as coincidence would have it, by the way, this was the original meaning of the Latin word "vagina!"). In this as in other matters, it is often advisable to humor your interlocutor with the impassible curiosity of an anthropologist instead of trying to convince him (it's usually a him!) with the facts.

The etymologies of all the roots surpass the scope of this introduction, particularly since some details are disputed; what is not seriously disputed is that they can all be traced to Proto-Slavic (that is, Indo-European) prototypes. For example, **хуй** is generally traced to a Proto-Balto-Slavic word meaning (pine) needle or thorn; it later assumed the meaning of "penis" during the Proto-Slavic stage (calling to mind the English term "prick"). The modern Russian word **хвоя**, meaning the needles of pine and fir trees, is derived from the same word. The fact that **хуй** has equivalents in almost every modern Slavic language, from Russian, Belarussian and Ukrainian (that is, East Slavic) to Polish and Czech (West Slavic) to Bulgarian (South Slavic) suggests that the word must trace its roots back to Proto-Slavic.

Meanwhile, certain **мат** words are attested in writing on so-called "birch-bark manuscripts" (**берестяные грамоты**, from the noun **береста**, meaning the bark that easily peels off of birch trees and was used as a kind of primitive note-paper once upon a time). These were found in the Novgorod region, and date as far back as 1100. Bark No. 531, dated to around 1200, was written by a woman (Anna) to her brother regarding some unjust accusations, and contains this passage (with no spaces between words):

сьтроумоюкоровоюидоцеребладею

If we modernize the spelling just a bit, this would read: [he called] "**сестру мою коровою и дочь блядью**" — "he called my sister a cow and my daughter a whore." As used in today's **мат**, the noun **блядь** would normally translate as "bitch," and we can see that people were calling each other bitches (and cows) almost a thousand years ago, at least! Bark No. 955, meanwhile — also from the 12th century — features the word **пизда**. To see for yourself, consult www.gramoty.ru. Inasmuch as the Mongol invasion began in 1237, we have hereby successfully dispensed with the "Mongol origin" theory of **мат**.

Why do they call it "мат," anyway?

Though I have heard other theories, the term **мат** seems ultimately to derive from **мать** (mother), on account of the all-important curse: **Ёб твою́ мать**. Although this is normally translated as "Fuck your mother," and means as much in present-day usage, its original meaning is more complicated, and will be discussed in detail later; it seems to have involved the pagan cult of the "damp mother earth." This Ur-curse and various accompanying obscenities came to be grouped under the category of **ма́терная брань**, which we might translate literally as "mother-related verbal abuse" (compare the verb **брани́ть / вы́бранить**, meaning "to scold, insult, abuse verbally").

Take a moment to note the obvious difference in pronunciation between **мать** (soft "t") and **мат** (hard "t") — this is a great pair to use when practicing softness, since in this case the hard/soft distinction is all that differentiates two completely different nouns! More on this and other issues of pronunciation in the following chapter. Note, by the way, that **мат** can also mean "mate" in chess.

A common synonym for **мат** is **матерщи́на**. A single word of **мат** is a **ма́терное сло́во** (the plural is **ма́терные слова́**). Another term, **матю́г**, meaning a word or expression of **мат**, is usually heard in the plural: **матюги́**. The latter figured memorably in late Soviet rock-bard Alexander Bashlachyov's song "**Вре́мя колоко́льчиков**" ("The Time of the Little Bells" — a kind of underground rock manifesto whose outstanding lyrics are worth checking out). In it, he sings of chewing **матюги́ с моли́твами** — "curses with prayers."

How does one talk about using мат in Russian?

The most common verb for "to curse" is **руга́ться / вы́ругаться**; to describe cursing using **мат** specifically, just use the instrumental case: **руга́ться ма́том**. For example: **Он ча́сто руга́ется ма́том** (He often curses using mat). Another common verb is the imperfective **мате́риться**, meaning "to curse" (in an ongoing, habitual, or repeated fashion). A related verb is the perfective **матюгну́ться** (also spelled **матюкну́ться**), meaning to let out a curse (once).

Note that in classical (19th-century and even most 20th-century) Russian literature these terms themselves — not to mention actual **мат** — are never found on the printed page. However, authors have ways of strongly implying an outburst of **мат**. Take the phrase: **крича́ть благи́м ма́том** (meaning something like "to scream bloody murder"), or calling someone "**тако́й и сяко́й**" ("this, that, and the other"). These suggest a barrage of unprintable words — perhaps including **мат**. Similar allusions to **мат** may be heard in everyday speech; for example, **хуй** (cock) may be referred to as the "**сло́во из трёх букв**," or one may speak of sending someone "**на три бу́квы**" ("onto three letters") — that is, **на хуй** ("onto a cock").

In literature published since the breakup of the Soviet Union, you can expect to see **мат** in print — in books by the likes of Vladimir Sorokin or Viktor Pelevin, to name just a couple. Indeed, their work can be all but impenetrable without knowledge of **мат**!

A note on Russian verb conjugation

Russian verb conjugation is quite complicated and can't possibly be covered fully here (for all the details, try the *Russian Through Propaganda* textbook).

In short, this book will mark each verb with a purely conventional "tag" indicating the conjugation pattern the verb follows (consult the table in the back of the book to see them all).

Each verb type takes one of two sets of endings, the "**и**" endings and the "**ё**" endings. Take two verbs we just learned, whose forms (present tense, imperative, and past tense) are presented below. The first, **ругаться**, is an **АЙ** verb (pronounced like "eye"); these verbs take "**ё**" endings. Meanwhile, **материться** is an **И** verb (pronounced like the "ee" in "seek"); these verbs take "**и**" endings. **АЙ** verbs and **И** verbs happen to be the most common types in Russian.

Furthermore, all verbs follow one of three stress patterns: 1) **stem** stress (the stress is fixed on some syllable in the stem; 2) **end** stress (the stress is always on the ending; or 3) **shifting** stress (the stress is on the *ending* of the first form (the "**я**" form), but shifts back to the *stem* in all remaining forms. In cases where the stress pattern can't be guessed from the infinitive (as is usually the case when the infinitive is stressed on the final syllable), it'll be given in superscript along with the type tag, e.g.: **материться** И^{end}. By the way, since **ругаться** is an **АЙ** verb, we know it's stem-stressed. Again — in short — it's complicated.

Both of the verbs below happen to be *reflexive*, adding the reflexive particle (**-ся**) after forms ending in a consonant, and its variant (**-сь**) after those ending in a vowel.

ругаться АЙ: to curse		материться И^{end}: to use mat	
руга**ю**сь	I curse	матер**ю**сь	I use mat
руга**ешь**ся	you curse	матер**ишь**ся	you use mat
руга**ет**ся	he / she curses	матер**ит**ся	he / she uses mat
руга**ем**ся	we curse	матер**им**ся	we use mat
руга**ете**сь	you curse	матер**ите**сь	you use mat
руга**ют**ся	they curse	матер**ят**ся	they use mat
руга**йся**!	curse!	матер**ись**!	use mat!
руга**л**ся	he cursed	матер**ил**ся	he used mat
руга**ла**сь	she cursed	матер**ила**сь	she used mat
руга**ли**сь	they cursed	матер**или**сь	they used mat

Who uses мат?

The question of who uses **мат**, and when, is a highly complex sociolinguistic topic. Though we can't presume to cover it fully, a few generalizations must be ventured. If, as we have seen, **мат** is regarded as "really bad language," then questions of its usage are certain to evoke a range of widely divergent and very forceful opinions.

Students of Russian will surely be exposed to these opinions in their interactions with native speakers — and while all opinions are valid as such, the opinion of any one native speaker should not be taken as authoritative. Beware in particular claims such as "No one *ever* says *that!*" or "One must never, ever say *that!*" — claims I've heard native Russian speakers make concerning words as innocent as the baby-talk verb **кушать** (to eat), which Russians of all stripes use constantly, but which, apparently, has failed to win the approval of certain sophisticates. So, one the one hand, we have the blanket claim that *no* dignified or educated person would *ever* use **кушать**, and, on the other, the undeniable fact that Russians most definitely *do use it*. I cite this purely by way of example.

This brings us to one opinion — masquerading as fact — that must be blown out of the water: the idea that "educated" or "cultured" Russians *never* use **мат**. This opinion holds that **мат** is spoken exclusively by the lower strata of society, and that its use immediately marks the speaker as some sort of cretin. Aside from being demonstrably false, this idea perhaps says more about the humorlessness and prudishness of those who propagate it than it does about the actual facts of usage. Some of the great masters of **мат** whom I've encountered personally have been highly educated people, with advanced degrees. Others, certainly, were not. But there's no necessary correlation between social standing and openness to **мат**. By analogy, we might ask whether an English speaker's level of education or cultural refinement necessarily correlates with his or her willingness to drop an occasional f-bomb when circumstances demand it.

With this important point out of the way, we must hasten to add that — obviously! — even those who do enjoy indulging in **мат** will do so with some level of discretion, and that an "educated" and "cultured" person is more likely to exercise such discretion than, say — I don't know — a drunken ex-convict or juvenile delinquent.

So, let's give a few sweeping generalizations of our own concerning who tends to use **мат**, and in what settings.

First, we should state the plain fact that although Russia has changed over recent decades and will presumably continue to change, it remains a relatively more traditional society when it comes to notions of gender roles, and to attitudes toward sex in general. The fact that **мат** roots refer exclusively to genitalia and intercourse — and not to defecation — is often interpreted as indicative of a long-standing taboo on all things sexual; moreover, the ancient oath at the heart of **мат** (may a dog fuck mother earth) invokes the sexual defilement of a maternal deity as the most horrible thing imaginable.

But without speculating as to the reasons, the simple fact is that **мат** has long been the domain of men, and, for the most part, remains so today. This certainly does not mean that women never use **мат**, but it does mean that 1) men are generally less likely to use **мат** in the presence of women, especially female family members, and especially mothers; and 2) the use of **мат** by women is generally more shocking and more subject to judgment.

It also means that **мат** is far more likely to be used in male-dominated social contexts — say, when playing or watching soccer, when drinking, or generally in conversation with male friends. In such contexts, the use of **мат** may signal real emotion (anger, frustration — or humor), or it may simply signal a kind of intimacy or sincerity — that one is freely saying what one really thinks to an understanding audience.

Generally, **мат** may be resorted to — even by those who'd rarely use it otherwise — to **называ́ть ве́щи свои́ми имена́ми** (to "call things by their names," i.e. "call a spade a spade"). When confronted by anything from horrific atrocities, to atrocious human beings, to the horrors of the human condition, there may be a sense that only **мат** is adequate to the phenomena one seeks to name. In such instances, even speakers too delicate (or too constrained by the social context) to use **мат** openly may allude to it without actually uttering it — either through some of the standard euphemisms we'll discuss later, or by some description of the word's spelling!

For example, instead of saying what everyone's thinking ("**Пизде́ц!**" — "We're fucked, this fucking sucks, this is a fucking disaster!"), they'll mention **одно́ сло́во на бу́кву "п"** (a certain word that starts with the letter "п"), followed by something like "**Зна́ете како́е, да?**" (You know which one, right?). Or, as we've seen, instead of sending someone **на́ ху́й** ("onto a cock"), they'll send them "**на три бу́квы**" ("onto three letters").

Finally, we should reiterate that the more formal or "polite" the context, the less likely **мат** is to be used. Even those who use it lustily among friends or even casual acquaintances would typically balk at using it with strangers, especially in formal circumstances — unless, of course, something outrageous forces them to make their true feelings known!

Should I use мат?

Um, probably not. At least, not until you have a lot of experience speaking Russian, and exposure to what language is used in what settings. Otherwise, you risk gravely offending someone, not to mention making a fool of yourself. Generally speaking, language learners should probably resist the urge to use too much slang or obscenity, which tend to require a high degree of both linguistic and cultural fluency before they can be deployed with aplomb. And, anyway, it's never a good idea to look like you're "trying too hard." Especially when you're dealing with something as explosive as **мат**.

That being said, there's no doubt that you'll win a lot of respect — even awe — among certain Russians for understanding some **мат**. And, in the right circumstances, a well-placed bit of **мат** from a non-native speaker can elicit amazement and delight. But, if you *do* decide to dabble in **мат**, keep two tips in mind.

First: you must gauge the setting and your interlocutor(s) very carefully before "going there." Err on the side of caution, and — better yet — wait until a native speaker has used **мат** him- or herself, thereby signaling that they are receptive to it and that the setting is appropriate. Usually, of course, this would be with close friends in informal situations.

Second: don't overdo it. Let's circle back to the purpose of this book: we're deliberately limiting ourselves to basic **мат** phrases and very simple examples — the kinds of things people often say, and that even a Russian learner can deploy with confidence and without overdoing things. And let's be honest: even among native speakers, **мат** is usually kept pretty simple, pretty uninventive. Certainly, a true virtuoso can string together diabolical concatenations of **мат** words, and perhaps even improvise a couple of new ones. If you spend time among Russians, you're bound to overhear, at some point, an epic **мат**-laced rant — even from a total stranger, in public (I can personally think of a handful of such incidents that left me and everyone present in tears of laughter). And the funniest outbursts, in my experience, are always "existential" in nature; that is, they're not just mindless insults, but lamentations.

But such performances are rare. So, keep it simple; start with the phrases in this book; and then build a more advanced **мат** vocabulary as you encounter new expressions in real life.

Where did this book come from?

This brings me to a final topic — a very telling one. When I first arrived in Russia, fresh out of college, I'd had roughly two years of formal study of Russian, and, thanks to quite a bit of independent study in preparation for my year in St. Petersburg, I was pretty well versed in Russian grammar and was beginning to read literature in the original. True, it would take some time for my speaking ability to develop... but the point is that I was reasonably familiar with the language.

On perhaps my third visit to Moscow to spend time with some Russian friends, who at the time were all students at Moscow State University, they had an impromptu vodka evening — just four of us sitting around a kitchen table. At some point I — and they — realized that I was not following the conversation *at all*. Why? Well, for no particular reason, they'd slipped into using **мат**.

When they realized my predicament, they grabbed a single piece of paper, and — delighted to share their insider knowledge with a foreigner — spent the next few hours compiling a list of basic **мат** terms, explaining each one — complete with simple examples and fulls sets of euphemisms. That very list — in expanded form — served as the basis of this book. This piece of paper was invaluable to me — I could now follow any conversation, understand music, read some recent literature, and, most importantly, appreciate a lot of humor — including some of the epic rants I just mentioned. All of this would have been completely inaccessible had native speakers not taken the time to explain **мат** to me.

So, I'm now passing the knowledge along in the form of this book! Enjoy!

The Russian Alphabet

To ensure that the joys of cursing are accessible for both seasoned students of Russian and complete beginners, let's begin with the Russian version of the Cyrillic alphabet, and the (informal) system of transliteration we'll be using in this book.

Even if you know the alphhabet already, you may benefit from being reminded that although Russian follows the "one letter = one sound" principle to a much greater degree than English, some letters can still represent more than one sound. All of the transliterations in this book will try to capture this as fully as possible; it may therefore be useful for learners of all levels to compare them to the Cyrillic original.

	usually:	sometimes:			usually:	sometimes:
А а	ah	uh		Р р	r	
Б б	b	p		С с	s	
В в	v	f		Т т	t	
Г г	g	k (or v*)		У у	oo	
Д д	d	t		Ф ф	f	
Е е	yeh	(y)ih		Х х	kh	
Ё ё	yoh			Ц ц	ts	
Ж ж	zh	sh		Ч ч	ch	
З з	z	s		Ш ш	sh	
И и	ee	i		Щ щ	shsh	
Й й	y (consonant)			Ъ ъ	hard sign (rare)	
К к	k			Ы ы	y (vowel)	
Л л	l			Ь ь	soft sign	
М м	m			Э э	eh	
Н н	n			Ю ю	yoo	
О о	oh	ah / uh		Я я	yah	(y)ih
П п	p					

* in "**его**" and "**ого**" only; see p. 21

Vowels

Four vowels are marked by two different letters — the second letter, called a "soft" vowel, typically begins with the sound of an English "y" (as in "yes"), or a Russian й.

А а	ah	"Open up and say '**ah**!'"	➡	**Я я**	yah	Like the ya in "**ya**cht."
Э э	eh	Short English "e," as in "s**e**t."	➡	**Е е**	yeh	Like the ye in "**ye**s."
О о	oh	Like the "o" in "m**o**re."	➡	**Ё ё**	yoh	Like "yo" in "**yo**re."
У у	oo	Like an owl: "**Hoo! Hoo!**"	➡	**Ю ю**	yoo	Think "**Yoo**-hoo!"

Using an "h" can be a helpful visual cue for English speakers trying to nail down some Russian vowels; for example, Russian "a" is like open up and say "**ah**!" — and never like the "**ay**" in "day," or anything else. But, our transliterations may drop the "h" if it seems too cumbersome. The next vowel is very easy to pronounce:

И и	ee	Like the "ee" in "f**ee**t."

Our final vowel, however, is *unlike anything in English*. To pronounce it, try positioning your tongue half-way between the positions used to say "ah" and "ee." Although this sound may seem to resemble the "**ooey**" in English "**gooey**," it (like all Russian vowels) is "pure" — that is, it consists of a single sound, not two sound blended together.

Ы ы	y	Try "**ooey**" as a *single* sound! This takes practice!

Finally, note that the letter **й** (not to be confused with **и**!) is a *consonant*, and is always preceded or followed by a vowel, my like English "y" (as in "boy" and "yoyo").

The combination **ый** (common in masculine adjectives) will be transliterated as "y":

ёбанный = YO-bun-ny   Fucking (literally, "fucked")

Russian Stress

Understanding stress is essential to Russian pronunciation — especially in certain **мат** expressions. Russian words place heavy, unmistakable emphasis on **one syllable only**. Which syllable in particular is not predictable, and is not ordinarily marked in "real" Russian texts. In this book, we'll mark stress in the Cyrillic by underlining the vowel in the stressed sylllable; in the transliteration, we'll CAPITALIZE the syllable:

пиздец = piz-DYETS   This fucking sucks!

Note that the letter **ё** can only occur in a stressed syllable:

ёбанный придурок = YO-bun-ny pri-DOO-ruhk   Fucking ("fucked") idiot!

In some cases a noun's stress may jump back onto a *preposition*. For example:

Пошёл на хуй! = pa-SHOL NA khuy!   Go fuck yourself!

Vowel Reduction

When a given Russian vowel happens not to occur in a stressed syllable, it may be pronounced differently. This means that a given vowel letter may represent more than one sound depending on where it occurs with respect to the stressed syllable.

The rules for this are somewhat complex, but since our transliterations will reflect how each vowel is *actually pronounced* (despite how it's spelled!) we needn't get into the details. Here are the vowels which are pronounced differently when unstressed; the first two ("**a**" and "**o**") are particularly noticeable, and therefore very important.

stressed: unstressed:

А а   ah   ah / uh   ➡   **ёбанная в ро̲т!**
                                  YO-bun-nuh-yuh v ROT! (fucked in the mouth!)

О о   oh   ah / uh   ➡   **пиздобо̲л**   **муди̲ло**
                                  piz-dah-BOL (a bullshitter)   moo-DEE-luh (asswipe)

When unstressed, the letter **и** can sound more like a short English "i" (as in "sit").

И и   ee   i   ➡   **пиз̲да̲**   **спи̲здить**
                          piz-DA (cunt)   SPEEZ-dit' (to steal)

Finally, these two letters can sound more like "yi" (or "i") — the "i" as in "**sit**."

Е е   yeh   (y)i   ➡   **Ты меня̲ заеба̲л!**
                              ty min-YA za-yi-BAL!   (I'm fucking sick of you!)

Я я   yah   (y)i   ➡   **Спи̲здят.**
                              SPEEZ-dyit.   (They'll fucking steal it.)

Hardness and softness

This is perhaps the most difficult feature of Russian pronunciation: many Russian consonants come in "hard" and "soft" variants. Because English consonants tend to be "hard," the "hard" versions of Russian consonants present no problem — that is, the hard Russian **н** is like the English "n," the hard Russian **т** is like the English "t," etc.

First, how do we know if a Russian consonant is soft? Well, we *assume it is* **hard** by default. By convention, a consonant is marked as **soft** if it is followed by these letters:

1) the vowel **и**;   2) the "soft vowels" **е, ё, ю, я**;   3) the "soft sign," **ь**

Compare the words **мат** (the vulgar language we're learning!) and **мать** (mother). The **т** in **мат** is hard; the **т** in **мать** is soft.

Or, compare the phrases **Пошёл на хуй!** (fuck off) and **Ни хуя себе!** (fucking wow!). The **н** in **на** is hard, but the **н** in **ни** is soft, since it's followed by an **и**.

In our transliterations, a consonant will be marked as soft if followed by a **y** (as in the soft vowels yeh, yoh, yoo, yah), by **i** (ee), or by an apostrophe (') marking a soft sign:

Пошёл на хуй!	Go fuck yourself!	(**hard "n"** in "na")
pa-SHOL NA khuy!		
Ни хуя себе!	Fucking wow!	(**soft "n"** in "ni")
ni khu-YA si-BYEH!		

Now that we know how Russian indicates soft consonants — how do we pronounce them? While this takes a *lot of practice*, the mechanics are pretty simple: your tongue must be in the position required to make the vowel **и** ("ee" in transliteration). Try it — this is the easy part! Now, keeping your tongue in that position, do whatever else you need to do to produce the given consonant — an "n," for example. The result should sound like the "n" in "onion" (without the following -on). Note that if you allow your tongue to drop back from its **и** ("ee") position, the result will be a hard consonant. Since English consonants tend toward hardness, this habit is very hard to overcome, and explains why pronouncinig soft consonants is such a challenge for English speakers. Of course, a detailed discussion of this is beyond the scope of this book — try a Russian textbook, or consult a native speaker (including on YouTube videos!).

Devoicing

Finally, you may have noticed that several consonants may also be pronounced differently in certain positions. The most conspicuous instance is "devoicing" of consonants that are the **final letter** in a word.

A consonant is "**voiced**" if our vocal cords are vibrating when we pronounce it. For example, "z" is voiced, but "s" is not. We can think of "z—s" as a voiced-unvoiced pair, in the sense that they are produced in the same way; the only difference is whether the sound is voiced or not.

A consonant that is normally **voiced** is pronounced as its **unvoiced** counterpart when it is the final letter in a word. That is, a final "z" is pronounced like an "s."

Again, our transliterations will try to capture this. Compare:

Ебись оно всё конём!   Let it all get fucked by a horse!
yi-BEES' ah-NO VSYO kah-NYOM!

Ёб твою мать!   Fuck you!
YOP tva-YOO MAT'!

The **б** in **Ебись** is pronounced like "b" (soft b, actually), while the final-position **б** in **Ёб** is devoiced to a "p." While similar changes can occur in consonant clusters, this word-final devoicing is by far the most important instance to watch for in this book.

Tricky Consonants

Most Russian consonants correspond fairly closely to their English equivalents, and don't require much explanation. For example, the Russian **д** corresponds to an English "d" — as long as we remember that 1) it may be devoiced to a **т**; and 2) it may be a soft "d," as in the combinations **дь, ди, де, дё, дю, дя**).

With this in mind, here is a summary of consonants that require a bit of discussion.

Й й   y   As mentioned above, this letter — though it sometimes confuses students — works exactly like an English "y" followed or preceeded by a vowel, as in "boy" or "yo-yo." In English, "y" can also represent a vowel, as in "by." In Russian, however, **й** is always a consonant, and cannot appear without an adjacent vowel.

Пошёл на хуй!   Go fuck yourself!
pa-SHOL NA khuy!

Again, remember that the letters **е, ё, ю, я** represent an **й** sound followed by a vowel.

Ебать!   Fuck!
yi-BAT'!

Р р   r   This is a trilled or rolled "r," and really sounds nothing like the English "r." It is made by flapping the tip of the tongue against the upper front teeth; if we take the English word "butter," the Russian "r" is actually closer to the "tt" than to the "r." Ideally, this flapping should be repeated, producing an extended, rolled "r" — especially when emphatically and lustily cursing! If you're not able to make this sound already, consult any number of videos on YouTube concerning how to "roll" or "trill" your R's. Don't give up if you can't do it at first; this *can* be learned with practice!

Ебись оно всё в рот!   Let it all get fucked in
yi-BEES' ah-NO VSYO v ROT!   the mouth.

Х х   kh   This is like the guttural, throat-clearing "ch" in the German name "Bach." Don't be shy with this — especially when cursing! Given the ubiquity of the word **хуй** (khuy) in Russian mat, this is a very important sound to master!

Хуй тебе!   Fuck you, I'm not giving
KHUY ti-BYEH!   you shit!

Ц ц   ts   Like the "ts" in "cats," this sound is not at all hard to pronounce, but learners sometimes struggle to think of it as a single letter that can occur anywhere in a word, including at the beginning.

пиздец   total fucking shit
piz-DYETS

Ни дня без пиздеца.   Not a day without shit.
nee DNYA byis piz-dyeh-TSA

Ш ш	sh

This is easy: like the "sh" in English "shit." Note that there is no distinction made between hard and soft **ш**; even if **ш** happens to be followed by a soft sign (**ь**), it is pronounced as usual. This is especially common in second-person singular verb endings:

Пиздишь.   You're talking bullshit.
piz-DEESH

Ч ч	ch

Also easy: like the "ch" in "chair." As with **ш**, there is no distinction between a hard and soft **ч**; even if **ч** happens to be followed by a soft sign (**ь**), it is pronounced as usual.

Хуячь!   Fucking shoot (hit, strike)!
khoo-YACH!

Ж ж	zh

Like the "s" in "pleasure" or the second "g" in "garage," this sound presents no difficulty. It can be devoiced to a "sh" sound, as in the English "Shh! Be quiet!"

пиздёж   Bullshit
piz-DYOSH

Я в жопу пьян.   I'm fucking wasted.
yah v ZHOH-poo P'YAN.

Щ щ	shsh

This letter essentially represents a **ш** ("sh"), held for twice the length. However, it occurs quite rarely, and will not be featured in any of our **мат** vocabulary!

The Hard Sign

We discussed already how to tell if a consonant is soft: if it is followed by one of these "soft" vowels (**и, е, ё, ю, я**) or the "soft sign" (**ь**). In all other cases, a consonant is simply *assumed to be hard*. For this reason, the "hard sign" (**ъ**) is quite rare in modern Russian; it is only used when a prefix ending in a hard consonant is added to a word that happens to begin with a soft vowel. Without an intervening hard sign, the resulting spelling would incorrectly suggest that the consonant was soft.

This is all a bit confusing, perhaps — but we will see very few examples of this. One is the verb **съёбываться** АЙ / **съебаться**: to get the fuck out.

Мне надо съебаться отсюда.   I've got to get the fuck out of here.
mnyeh NAH-duh syeh-BAHT-suh aht-SYOO-duh.

A Crash Course in Russian Verbs

Russian verbs are complicated, and a fulll description is far beyond the reach of this book. But some brief notes on our approach to verbs are in order.

Russian has only **three tenses**; while past-tense forms (whose endings typically include -**л**) are relatively easy — usually formed from the verb's infinitive — other forms conjugate according to a number of patterns.

As we noted earlier, this book will formally present every verb by giving its **infinitive**, followed by a "**tag**" indicating its conjugation type. A full table of these types can be found in the back of the book. Note that these tags are for learning purposes only, and are purely conventional; they are not used by Russians! Here's a sample entry:

блядничать АЙ: to act like a bitch (like а **блядь**)

This tells us that this verb conjugates according to the АЙ pattern, for which the model verb in the reference table is **читать** АЙ. This implies the following:

читать АЙ: to read			**блядничать** АЙ: to act like a bitch	
я	чит**аю**	I read	блядничаю	I act like a bitch
ты	чит**аешь**	you read	блядничаешь	you act like a bitch
он, она, оно	чит**ает**	he, she, it reads	блядничает	he, she acts like a bitch
мы	чит**аем**	we read	блядничаем	we act like bitches
вы	чит**аете**	you read	блядничаете	you act like bitches
они	чит**ают**	they read	блядничают	they act like bitches

Unlike **блядничать**, which has only one infinitive, the vast majority of Russian verbs come in pairs of infinitives, called **aspectual pairs**. As cited in this book, the first infinitive has "imperfective" aspect, while the second has "perfective" aspect. Here's a typical entry, with translations that capture the basic aspectual distinction:

спиздывать АЙ / **спиздить** И: to fucking steal

спиздывать (imperfective): to fucking steal (generally), to be in the process of stealing; to steal repeatedly or habitually; to be attempting to steal

спиздить И: to fucking steal (with emphasis on result), to steal completely, to steal once, to steal successfully

The conjugation patterns are as follows. Note that when we conjugate a **perfective** verb, the resulting forms are **future**-tense in meaning:

спиздывать АЙ: to steal (imperfective)		**спиздить** И: to steal (perfective)	
спиздываю	I fucking steal	спиз**жу**	I'll fucking steal
спиздыва**ешь**	you fucking steal	спизд**ишь**	you'll fucking steal
спиздыва**ет**	he / she fucking steals	спизд**ит**	he / she'll fucking steal
спиздыва**ем**	we fucking steal	спизд**им**	we'll fucking steal
спиздыва**ете**	you fucking steal	спизд**ите**	you'll fucking steal
спиздыва**ют**	they fucking steal	спизд**ят**	they'll fucking steal

If an infinitive is given with no "tag," this means that it's **irregular**; its conjugation pattern doesn't quite match up with any of the types. Such verbs are very few.

Aspect is an essential and pervasive feature of Russian; almost every time one uses a verb in Russian, one must choose between its imperfective and perfective form, depending on the context and on what one wishes to emphasize within that context. Because English grammar lacks aspect in this systematic sense, aspect is one of the most difficult parts of learning Russian — and we can only scratch the surface in this book. We'll explain additional details as we come to them.

Next, we should note how the **two forms of "you"** are used in Russian. The pronoun **ты** (ty), and all of its verb forms, is used to address a single person informally or familiarly. These forms are used with family members, close friends, pets, God, etc. The pronoun **вы** (vy), and all of its verb forms, is, first of all, the plural "you" (think English "you all", "y'all," "you guys," etc.) — so, it can be used to address **multiple** people, whether informally or formally (politely) — and to address a **single** person formally.

Because so many **мат** expressions are inherently insulting (and certainly "informal!"), they're heard most often in their **ты** forms when addressing a "you." But the **вы** forms may still be heard — certainly when addressing multiple people, or, on occasion, when addressing a single "you" politely (often with an air of sarcasm).

For examples, let's take another important verb form: the **imperative** (used for giving commands). The rules for forming the **ты** imperative are complex, and can't be covered here; they'll simply be provided. But, if we know the **ты** imperative, we can always form the **вы** imperative by simply adding -**те** (-tye). We can negate any imperative (telling people not to do something) by adding the negative **не**. If the verb is reflexive, add the particle -**ся** (-сь) on at the end:

Не руга́йся!
nyeh roo-GAHY-syuh!

Don't curse!
(informally, to one person)

Не руга́йтесь!
nyeh roo-GAHY-tyes'!

Don't curse!
(to multiple people, or formally to one person)

We should note that when a person who should be addressed formally (a stranger, a superior, an elder, etc.) is addressed using the informal **ты**, this is itself inherently **insulting** — quite aside from whatever offensive **мат** expression is being used.

A Crash Course in Russian Nouns and Adjectives

Russian is also made difficult by its extensive use of **inflection** — that is, changing the **endings** (the "case" endings) of nouns and adjectives based on the role they play in a sentence. Without delving further into this topic here, simply note that nouns and adjectives will first be given in their basic forms, as in a dictionary — the nominative singular for nouns, and the masculine singular for adjectives. But you'll notice that these forms will often change in any particular expression. For example:

пизда   pussy, cunt (here in the nominative singular)
piz-DAH

Иди в пизду!   Fuck off, go into the pussy! (in the accusative singular,
i-DEE fpiz-DOO   expressing "motion into" following the preposition **в**)

хуй   dick, cock
khuy

Пошёл на хуй!   Fuck off, go onto a cock! (accusative singular, which
pa-SHOL NA khuy!   for this masculine noun is the same as the nominative)

У нас нет ни хуя.   We don't have a fucking thing. (genitive singular,
OO nas nyet ni khu-YA.   expressing "non-existence" with **нет**)

As these examples show, many uses of case endings are determined by **preposi-tions**; all prepositions in Russian simple "take" certain cases. In terms of pronuncia-tion, even experienced Russian learners should pay special attention to prepositions that consist of a single consonant only, like **в** (v). Since these have no vowel of their own, they must be pronounced *as if they were a part of the word that follows* — with **no pause** *whatsoever*. Indeed, read the preposition and the word that follows just as if they were in fact *a single word* — without a space in between!

When we do this, and the sound of the preposition's consonant blends into the initial sound of the word that follows, we may see **assimilation** — that is, the preposition's consonant may "become similar" to the consonant that follows in terms of being voiced / devoiced. The most noticeable phenonemon in this regard is **devoicing in consonant clusters**. For example, if the preposition **в** (v) — normally *voiced* — is immediately followed by an unvoiced consonant like **п** (p), then it will be pronounced like its *unvoiced* equivalent — in this case, **ф** (f).

Again, this topic is somewhat complex — but for the purposes of this book, keep in mind that the transliterations will attempt to capture the actual pronunciation. Return to the example "**Иди в пизду!**" and note carefully how the **в** is transliterated as "f" (not "v!"), and is written as one word with the following noun. If you're reading the Cy-rillic, be sure that you're actually pronouncing it in this way — this is a very important point of Russian pronunciation that is often ignored even by fairly advanced students.

Иди в пизду!   Fuck off, go into the pussy!
i-DEE fpiz-DOO

The same assimilation occurs with longer prepositions that end in a consonant:

Ни дня без пиздеца.   Not a day without shit.
nee DNYA byis piz-dyeh-TSA

Russian г sometimes sounds like English "v"

Returning to consonants for a moment, note that the Russian **г** (g) is pronounced exactly like **в** (v) in certain words involving the form **его** (yi-VOH), which can mean "him" or "his." Here again, the transliterations will reflect this. For example:

Я посла́л его́ на хуй.
yah pa-SLAL yi-VO NA khuy.

I told him to fuck off ("sent him onto the cock").

Хуй его́ зна́ет.
KHUY yi-VOH ZNA-yet.

Who the fuck knows. ("Dick knows it.")

This is also true of the masculine and neuter genitive singular ending of adjectives — "**-ого**." We won't be seeing this ending in many of our basic **мат** expressions.

Review and Practice

Here are just a few expressions to review. Keep in mind that the transliterations used here are only approximate, and conceived as the most convenient for readers who haven't mastered Cyrillic; they do not reflect any "official" system of transliteration. But, again, even seasoned students of Russian may benefit by comparing a word's Cyrillic spelliing with its actual pronunciation, as suggested by the transliteration — be sure you're reducing your vowels and devoicing your consonants correctly.

Note that the translations given here are simply rough English equivalents that reflect how the Russian expression is used, and not necessarily its literal meaning. We'll explain both the literal meanings and uses of all these expressions as we come to them.

Watch in particular for: 1) reduction of vowels; 2) devoicing of consonants; 3) soft consonants; and — always! — 4) STRESS!

Пошёл на хуй!
pa-SHOL NA khooy!

Go fuck yourself!

(note how **по-** is pronounced "pah")

Иди на хуй!
i-DEE NA khooy!

Go fuck yourself!

(note the soft "d")

мудило
moo-DEE-luh

Asswipe! Nutsack!

(note how the -**о** is pronounced "uh")

Мне всё по хуй.
mnyeh vsyo PO khuy.

I don't give a fuck about anything.

(note how the stress has shifted to the preposition **по**)

Ёб твою́ мать!
YOP tva-YOO MAT'!

Fuck you!

(note the soft **т**, and the, devoicing of **б** to **п**)

When people think of **мат**, this is likely the first word that comes to mind. Literally, it refers to the male reproductive organ; but, as is typical of **мат**, it can also be used as a root for building a wide variety of word with a range of meanings, many of which have no literal connection with the reproductive organ. Much like "four-letter words" in English, **хуй** (khuy) is referred to euphemistically as the "word of three letters":

сло̲во из трёх букв SLO-vuh is TRYOKH BOOKF	the word (consisting of) of three letters

One may even hear this substitution made in actual **мат** phrases — for example:

Я посла̲л его̲ на̲ хуй. ya pa-SLAL yi-VO NA khuy.	I told him to fuck off ("I sent him onto the cock.")
Я посла̲л его̲ на три бу̲квы. ya pa-SLAL yi-VO na TREE BOOK-vy	I "sent him onto the three letters."

Speaking of euphemisms, we've come already to one of the most essential points of understanding **мат** — namely, the system of euphemistic substitutions of harmless roots for the extremely vulgar root **хуй**. As we've discussed already, actual **мат** expressions are generally considered far more obscene than English curse words — but that doesn't mean that **мат** expressions are never heard in casual, even semi-formal speech. They are! But odds are that one of three euphemistic roots will be substitued wherever **хуй** would appear if one were *really* cursing.

Hence, we have the four following roots, in order of descending obscenity:

Why these roots? Well, the first two are clearly used because of their initial letter — a sound that inevitably conjures up that unmentionable **хуй**. The word **хер** is actually the old (Church Slavonic) name for the Cyrillic letter **х**. Meanwhile, the word **хрен** means, literally, "horseradish." Obviously, the literal meaning of these words has nothing to do with their use as euphemisms for **хуй**; it's all about the sound.

The final word, **фиг**, bears no phonic resemblence whatsoever to **хуй**, which helps explain why it's by far the mildest of these four forms — indeed, one hears **фиг** expressions all the time, in all but the most formal situations, and although everyone would understand how they point to actual **мат** expressions, few would find them offensive. Understood literally, **фиг** can refer both to a fig (the fruit) and to an obscene gesture, roughly equivalent in meaning to the "middle finger." The gesture is made by clenching one's fist with the thumb protruding between the index and middle fingers.

It must be said that **хер** expressions are relatively rare; in certain expressions, this root is hardly ever heard at all. Although any serious student of **мат** should be aware of **хер**, you can think of **хрен** as your go-to euphemism when you want a hint of vulgarity, and use **фиг** when you want to "make your feelings known" in harmless fashion. But remember that even **фиг** expressions should never, ever be used in formal contexts, or with anyone whose tolerance for edgy language is in question.

Let's take the most common **хуй** expression and see how this substition works:

Пошёл на хуй!	Go fuck yourself, "Go onto a cock."
pa-SHOL NA khooy	(said to a single guy, using **ты**)

Note how the preposition **на** is stressed — while the noun **хуй** has no stress! Such shifting of stress from an object of a preposition onto the preposition itself happens in certain set expressions in Russian (for example: **Карандаш упал на пол**. The pencil fell to the floor). This is *extremely* important for pronouncing this phrase correctly!

Now, let's substitute all three euphemisms. Note carefully how the meaning remains essentially unchanged — all that changes is the degree of vulgarity!

Пошёл на хер!	**Пошёл на хрен!**	**Пошёл на фиг!**
pa-SHOL NA kher	pa-SHOL NA khren	pa-SHOL NA fig

Because these substitutions are so common, we'll include all such variations in the examples below. Remember: **хер** is relatively rare, but in theory always possible. But you can rest assured that the **хрен** and **фиг** variants are widely used in every expression listed here.

Go fuck yourself, fuck off! / Пошёл н**а** хуй!

When speaking to a single **male**, say:

Пошёл на хуй!	**Пошёл на хер!**	**Пошёл на хрен!**	**Пошёл на фиг!**
pa-SHOL NA khuy	pa-SHOL NA kher	pa-SHOL NA khren	pa-SHOL NA fig

The past-tense form of the verb here (**пошёл**) has the sense of an urgent command — not "You went," but something like "Go, already!" Compare the common expressions **Пошл**и! (Let's get going!) or **Пое**хали! (Let's get rolling — by vehicle, that is!).

If speaking to a single **female**, you'll need the feminine verb forms:

Пошла **на хуй!**	**Пошл**а **на хер!**	**Пошл**а **на хрен!**	**Пошл**а **на фиг!**
pa-SHLA NA khuy	pa-SHLA NA kher	pa-SHLA NA khren	pa-SHLA NA fig

Finally, speaking to multiple people, or formally (!) to one person of any gender, say:

Пошли **на хуй!**	**Пошл**и **на хер!**	**Пошл**и **на хрен!**	**Пошл**и **на фиг!**
pa-SHLEE NA khuy	pa-SHLEE NA kher	pa-SHLEE NA khren	pa-SHLEE NA fig

Go fuck yourself, fuck off! / Ид**и** н**а** хуй!

Here's another way to say the same thing, using an ordinary imperative form:

to one person:	**Ид**и **на хуй!**	*to multiple people:*	**Ид**и**те на хуй!**
	i-DEE NA khuy		i-DEE-tyeh NA khuy

Telling someone to fuck off / посл**а**ть н**а** хуй

We've just learned two ways to "send someone..." The verb for this action is **посыл**а**ть** АЙ / **посл**а**ть** А. It's most often heard in the past tense:

Я посла**л ег**о **/ е**ё **/ их н**а **хуй.**	I sent him / her / them onto a cock.
ya pa-SLAL yi-VO / yi-YO / eekh NA khooy	(said by a male speaker)

Я посла**ла ег**о **/ е**ё **/ их н**а **хуй.**	I sent him / her / them onto a cock.
ya pa-SLAL-uh yi-VO / yi-YO / eekh NA khooy	(said by a female speaker)

We can also used it as an imperative, as in, "Tell him to go fuck himself!"

Пошли **ег**о **/ е**ё **/ их н**а **хуй.**	Send him / her / them onto a cock.
pa-SHLEE yi-VO / yi-YO / eekh NA khuy	(said to one person, informally)

One may hear an alternate (unprefixed) imperfective — **слать** A — used:

Шли всех на̱ хуй.	Send everyone onto a cock.
shlee fsyekh NA khuy	(said to one person, informally)

Here are the forms for the verb **посыла̱ть** АЙ / **посла̱ть** A. All "A" verbs show a mutation in all forms — in this case, the unusual cluster mutation **сл → шль**.

посыла̱ть АЙ: to send (imperfective)		**посла̱ть** A: to send (perfective)	
посыла̱ю	I send	пошлю̱	I will send
посыла̱ешь	you send	пошлёшь	you will send
посыла̱ет	he / she sends	пошлёт	he / she will send
посыла̱ем	we send	пошлём	we will send
посыла̱ете	you send	пошлёте	you will send
посыла̱ют	they send	пошлю̱т	they will send
посыла̱й!	send!	пошли̱!	send!
посыла̱л	he sent	посла̱л	he sent
посыла̱ла	she sent	посла̱ла	she sent
посыла̱ли	they sent	посла̱ли	they sent

Again, as sometimes happens, the basic unprefixed form **слать** A competes the (derived) pefixed imperfective **посыла̱ть** АЙ. They are essentially synonymous.

Lay a dick on that / Положи̱ хуй на э̱то!

This is an imperative of the verb **класть** Дᵉⁿᵈ / **положи̱ть** Иˢʰⁱᶠᵗ, meaning "to put into a lying position," or "lay," followed by "onto" with the accusative case.

Положи̱ хуй на э̱то.	Lay a dick on that, fuck that, forget it.
puh-lah-ZHEE khooy na eh-tuh	(said to one person, informally)

Note that euphemisms like **фиг** are *not* used in this expression! Here are the forms the aspectual pair — although this phrase is usually heard in the perfective.

класть Дᵉⁿᵈ: to lay (imperfective)		**положи̱ть** Иˢʰⁱᶠᵗ: to lay (perfective)	
кладу̱	I lay	положу̱	I will lay
кладёшь	you lay	поло̱жишь	you will lay
кладёт	he / she lay	поло̱жит	he / she will lay
кладём	we lay	поло̱жим	we will lay
кладёте	you lay	поло̱жите	you will lay
кладу̱т	they lay	поло̱жат	they will lay
клади̱!	lay!	положи̱!	lay!
кла̱л	he laid	положи̱л	he laid
кла̱ла	she laid	положи̱ла	she laid
кла̱ли	they laid	положи̱ли	they laid

You can all go fuck yourselves / Пошл<u>и</u> вы все н<u>а</u> хуй!

Here's a quick but extremely useful variation on an earlier constuction. As you may have noticed, the past plural of **пойти** (to go) — **пошли** — happens to be identical to the imperative of **послать** (to send). Here, we're back to the form of **пойти**: "go!"

Пошл<u>и</u> вы все н<u>а</u> хуй!
pa-SHLEE vy vsyeh NA khooy

Everyone fuck off, go onto a cock
(said to multiple people)

Here again, we can use the full range of euphemisms: **н<u>а</u> хер, н<u>а</u> хрен, н<u>а</u> фиг**.

More on euphemism...

You can actually tell a person to go fuck themselves without actually using a single word of **мат**. Although one might interpret "**Пошёл ты**" as nothing more than a brusque expression meaning "Get out" or "Away with you," the full **мат** expression **Пошёл (ты) на хуй** is so strongly implied that this phrase — even without the **хуй** — is extremely insulting. We will see other perhaps "innocent" expressions that are so strongly associated with **мат** that they are best avoided, unless you *want* to start a bar fight!

Fuck him, to hell with him / Хуй с ним!

This expression of indifference means, literally, "dick with" someone — as in, fuck them, I don't care what becomes of them. As is the case with many **мат** expressions, this one recalls the non-**мат** expressions "**Бог с ним**" (God be with him) and "**Чёрт с ним**" (The devil be with him). Literally, the former (with God) may be a blessing, and the latter a curse, but both can also express indifference.

Nouns or pronouns used after **с** ("with") requires the instrumental case. For example:

Хуй с ним!   Fuck him! Dick with him!
KHOOY s neem

Хуй с ней!   Fuck her! Dick with her!
KHOOY s nyey

Хуй с ними!   Fuck them! Dick with them!
KHOOY s NEE-mi

Хуй с тобой!   Fuck you! Dick with you!
KHOOY s tah-BOY   *(said to one person)*

Who the fuck knows / Хуй знает!

This phrase is an obscene way of saying, "Who knows?" — often in a dismissive tone. Compare the phrases "**Бог знает**" (God knows) or "**Чёрт знает**" (the devil knows).

Хуй знает!   Who the fuck knows! Dick knows!
KHOOY ZNA-yit

Like "**Бог знает**" or "**Чёрт знает**," this phrase can appear with indirect questions, or be combined with question words to express disbelief, dismissal, etc. For example:

Хуй знает, что он там делает.   Dick knows what he does there.
KHOOY ZNA-yit, CHTO on tam DYEH-luh-yit

Живёт он хуй знает где.   He lives dick knows where.
zhi-VYOT on KHOOY ZNA-yit GDYE

This phrase can also throw in a pronoun, in the accusative case, referring to who or what is being talked about. A few possible translations are given here:

Хуй е<u>го</u> зн<u>а</u>ет.   Dick knows what his deal is.
KHOOY yi-VO ZNA-yit

Хуй е<u>ё</u> зн<u>а</u>ет.   Dick knows what her problem is.
KHOOY yi-YO ZNA-yit

Хуй их зн<u>а</u>ет.   Dick knows what they're thinking.
KHOOY ikh ZNA-yit

The euphemisms **хер**, **хрен** and **фиг** are often substituted for **хуй**.

Fuck off, I'm not giving you shit / Хуй теб<u>е</u>!

In this simple phrase, **хуй** (in the accusative) combines with an indirect object in the dative case. In case you need to review, the dative forms of pronouns are: **мне** (to me; "mnyeh"), **тебе** (to you, informal; "ti-BYEH"), **ему** (to him; "yi-MOO"), **ей** (to her; "yey"), **нам** (to us; "nam"), **вам** (to you, plural or formal singular; "vam"), and **им** (to them, "eem").

Хуй теб<u>е</u>!   You get shit! You get dick!
KHOOY ti-BYEH

The euphemisms **хер**, **хрен** and **фиг** can all be substituted for **хуй**.

I don't give a fuck about that / П<u>о</u>хуй!

This is one of the most common and most important **мат** expressions. As is often the case, the literal meaning is somewhat obscured, and in any case rarely thought about — but it seems to derive from the idea of being "at cock level," or "up to the position of the cock." Hence, we might roughly compare it to phrases like "Fuck that" or, more literally, "I could fuck that." Compare other such constructions in Russian with **по** describing things that are "up to" some part of the body, such as: "**Снег по п<u>оя</u>с**" (snow up to my belt), or "**Я сыт по г<u>о</u>рло**" (I'm full (with food) up to my neck).

The expression **п<u>о</u>хуй** and its euphemistic variants are typically written as one word: **п<u>о</u>хуй**, **п<u>о</u>хер**, **п<u>о</u>хрен**, **п<u>о</u>фиг**. There are also (less common) forms using the dative with **по**: **п<u>о</u> хую**, **п<u>о</u> херу**, **п<u>о</u> хрену**, **п<u>о</u> фигу**. In all of these expressions, regardless of the case used, the preposition **по** is *always stressed*.

To tell who doesn't give a fuck, use the dative. To tell *what* they don't give a fuck about, use the nominative case. Examples:

П<u>о</u>хуй.   Fuck that. Who gives a fuck.
PO-khooy

(Мне) всё п<u>о</u>хуй. (mnyeh) vsyo PO-khooy	(I) don't give a fuck about anything. *(substitute other dative pronouns!)*
Нам п<u>о</u>хуй (в<u>а</u>ши угр<u>о</u>зы). nam PO-khooy (VA-shi oo-GRO-zy	We don't give a fuck about (your threats). *(substitute other nominative nouns!)*
Мне п<u>о</u>хуй, (чт<u>о</u> он д<u>у</u>мает). mnyeh PO-khooy (chto on DOO-ma-yit)	I don't give a fuck (what he thinks). *(substitute other question clauses!)*

A person who doesn't give a fuck / поху<u>и</u>ст

A couple of highly descriptive nouns are derived from the expression **похуй**. The first uses the suffix **-ист**, denoting a person belonging to a certain trade or ideology (compare **журнал<u>и</u>ст**: journalist, or **коммун<u>и</u>ст**: Communist): hence, **похуист**. Literally, this person takes life "at dick level." The term conveys a general sense of indifference, cynicim, or carelessness — something like the English "slacker."

We can swap out the root to obtain the following euphemisms:

поху<u>и</u>ст	похер<u>и</u>ст	похрен<u>и</u>ст	пофиг<u>и</u>ст
puh-khoo-EEST	puh-kher-EEST	puh-khren-EEST	puh-fig-EEST

Masculine nouns in **-ист** tend to have feminine equivalents in **-<u>и</u>стка**. Though relatively uncommon, feminines like **поху<u>и</u>стка** or **пофиг<u>и</u>стка** certainly do exist!

Ем<u>у</u> всё п<u>о</u>хуй. Он поху<u>и</u>ст. yi-MOO vsyo PO-khooy. On puh-khoo-EEST	He doesn't give a fuck about anything. He's a "don't-give-a-fuck-ist."

Not giving a fuck as a way of life / поху<u>и</u>зм

While nouns in **-ист** describe a devotee of a certain ideology, corresponding nouns in **-изм** denote that ideology (think **коммун<u>и</u>ст**: Communist → **коммун<u>и</u>зм**: Communism). Thus: **похуист**: a "don't-give-a-fuck-ist" → **похуизм**: "don't-give-a-fuck-ism" (that is, the behavior or worldview of a **похуист**). Again, a rough English equivalent might be "slackerism."

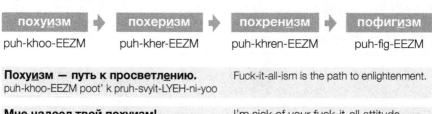

поху<u>и</u>зм	похер<u>и</u>зм	похрен<u>и</u>зм	пофиг<u>и</u>зм
puh-khoo-EEZM	puh-kher-EEZM	puh-khren-EEZM	puh-fig-EEZM

Поху<u>и</u>зм — путь к просветл<u>е</u>нию. puh-khoo-EEZM poot' k pruh-svyit-LYEH-ni-yoo	Fuck-it-all-ism is the path to enlightenment.
Мне надо<u>е</u>л твой поху<u>и</u>зм! mnyeh na-da-YEL tvoy puh-khoo-EEZM	I'm sick of your fuck-it-all attitude.

I don't fucking care / один хуй

This is a much less common way to express indifference than **похуй**. It also uses the dative case — to say, literally, that something "is the same dick" or "one dick" to someone. Compare the non-**мат** expression **всё равно** (it's all the same).

Мне один хуй, где сидеть. mnyeh ah-DEEN khooy, gdye si-DYET'	I don't give a fuck where we sit.

КОШКА У МЕНЯ БОЛЬШАЯ ПОФИГИСТКА!

Nothing whatsofuckingever / хуй

We saw earlier that the phrase **Хуй теб<u>е</u>** (literally, "dick to you") can mean something like "Get lost, I'm not giving you shit." Speaking more generally, **хуй** can serve as an emphatic stand-in for **нич<u>е</u>го**, in the emphatic sense of "nothing (whatsoever)." But note that the verbs in the expressions below (**ни хуя**) are not negated: to express the idea of "You won't find anything," we're saying, literally, "You'll find dick" — not "You won't find dick" with the double negation we usually expect from Russian. In this respect, compare the expressions below with the following entry (**ни хуя**).

As expected, we can replace **хуй** with the euphemisms **хер**, **хрен**, and **фиг**.

Хуй там найд<u>ё</u>шь. khooy tam nay-DYOSH	"You'll find dick (= nothing) there."
Хуй пол<u>у</u>чишь. khooy pa-LOO-chish	"You'll receive / get dick (= nothing)."

Nothing whatsofuckingever / ни хуя

Much more common are double-negated expressions with **ни** followed by the genitive (which is common in expressions of non-existence or with objects of negated verbs). These **мат** expressions are precise equivalents of **нич<u>е</u>го**, and can describe having nothing, or no amount of something. These expressions are extremely common.

ни хуя	ни хера	ни хрена	ни фига
ni khoo-YAH	ni khi-RAH	ni khri-NAH	ni fi-GAH

Again, note how the verbs too are negated, as they would be with **нич<u>е</u>го**.

Ни хуя не понима<u>ю</u>. nee khoo-YAH nye puh-ni-MA-yoo	I don't understand dick.
Он<u>и</u> там ни хуя не делают. ah-NEE tam ni khoo-YA nye DYEH-luh-yoot	They're not doing shit over there.
Нет у мен<u>я</u> ни хуя. nyet oo mi-NYAH ni khoo-YA	I don't have a single fucking thing.
П<u>и</u>ва у них нет ни хуя. PEE-vuh oo nikh nyet ni khoo-YA	They don't have shit for beer.
Ты ни хуя не сделал. ty ni khoo-YAH nye ZDYEH-luhl	You haven't gotten shit done.
Ни хуя не видно. ni khoo-YAH nye VEED-nuh	I can't see shit.

This phrase can be used adverbially in sense of "not at all" (**нисколько**).

Я ни хуя не удивлён.   I'm not surprised one fucking bit.
ya ni khoo-YAH nye oo-div-LYON

Note the common variant of **нет** — **нету**. It may imply that you don't have something with you at the moment, or being out of it, as opposed to lacking it altogether.

Нету денег ни хуя.   There's no fucking money.
NYEH-too DYEH-nig ni khoo-YA

Fucking unbelievable! / Ни хуя себе!

You've probably heard the phrase "**Ничего себе!**" It expresses great surprise or amazement, like the English "Wow!" Here too — as we might guess — we can re-place **ничего** with its **мат** equivalent: **ни хуя** (or one of its euphemisms).

— **Зенит победил со счётом 15-0.**   "Zenit won 15-0."
— **Ни хуя себе!**   "You must be fucking kidding me!"

— zi-NEET puh-byi-DEEL suh SHCHO-tom pyat-NA-tsat' nol'.
— ni khoo-YA si-BYEH!

— **Ни хуя себе пиво!**   "This beer is fucking unbelievable!"
— ni-khoo-YA si-BYEH PEE-vuh!

A shit ton of... / до ху**я**

A given **мат** root can yield a wide variety of words, with a range of meetings. Some may even be *antonyms* of sorts. While **ни хуя** expresses the idea of "none at all," the phrase **до хуя** describes having a shitload of something — a sufficient amount at the very least, if not overflowing bounty. Literally: "(all the way) to the dick."

Because we're speaking of a quantity "of" something, any nouns combined this phrase should be in the genitive case.

до ху**я** ⇒	до хер**а** ⇒	до хрен**а** ⇒	до фиг**а**
dah khoo-YAH	dah khi-RAH	dah khri-NAH	dah fi-GAH

So, the nouns below can all be replaced with other nouns in the genitive.

Пи**ва у нас до ху**я**.**
PEE-vuh oo nas dah khoo-YAH

"We've got a shitload of beer."

У меня **дел до ху**я**.**
oo mi-NYAH dyel dah khoo-YAH.

"I've got shit tons of work."

Де**нег у него до ху**я**.**
DYEH-nig oo nyi-VO dah khoo-YAH

"He's got shitloads of money."

What the fuck for? / на ху**я**?

The expression **на хуя** could be described as an extremely emphatic version of **почему**, **зачем**, or **на что**? — Why? What for? For what purpose? The thing whose purpose you're questioning appears in the nominative, and the person "for whom" it has no purpose is in the dative. Here's the usual set of euphemisms:

ТОВАРИЩИ!
ДЕЛ У НАС
ДО ХУЯ!

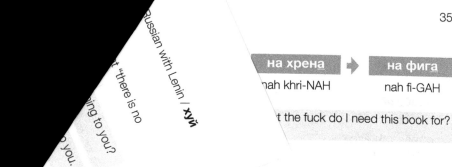

на хрен**а** ➡	на фиг**а**
...ah khri-NAH	nah fi-GAH

...t the fuck do I need this book for?

...gnly, "my dick") can express anything from bewilderment
... identical in meaning, but milder, is the phrase **ё-моё** — mild-
... that it doesn't explicitly invoke **хуй**. But note how even in **ё-моё** the
... invokes, by sound association, **ёб** (as in: **ёб твою мать!**). This accounts
... a range of euphemisms you may hear — for example, the even milder interjection
ёлки-палки; on par with such harmless and slightly goofy English expressions as
"fiddlesticks," it literally means "fir-tree sticks" (**ёлка** = fir tree, **палка** = stick).

Generally speaking, almost any word that happens to begin with **ху-** or **ё-** can easily
trigger associations with **мат**. The same goes for entire phrases that bears any phonic
resemblance to a **мат** phrase. To take one example that seems to have become
common around the time of the Russo-Japanese War (1904-05), the interjection
"**Япона мать!**" can stand in for "**Ёб твою мать!**" (or, more precisely, "**Ебёна
мать!**") — and reminds us yet again how easily the word **мать** (mother) can itself be
suggestive of the **мат** expression. Believe it or not, **Япона мать** (or Япона м**а**ма) has
served as the name of a sushi chain in Russia.

No euphemisms with **хер**, **хрен** or **фиг** are possible with these expressions.

Хуё-моё! Опять дождь!
khoo-YO-ma-YO! ah-PYAT' dozht'

Oh, for fuck's sake, it's raining again!

Ё-моё, машина опять сломалась!
YO-mah-YO, ma-SHEE-nuh ah-PYAT' sla-MA-las'

Oh, fuck me, the car broke down again!

The phrase **хуё-моё** can also stand in for phrases such as "this, that and the other"
(**и то и сё**), here and there (**туда-сюда**), etc.

Marking a question / ху́ли

The expression **ху́ли** is essentially a **мат** question word. It presumably arose from
хуй ли — **хуй** plus the interrogative particle **ли**, which, in addition to meaning
"whether," can simply mark a question, much like an ordinary question mark. Questions with **ху́ли** usually ask "why," or, more emphatically, "why the hell?"

Хули ты меня не любишь?
KHOO-li ty mi-NYAH nye LYOO-bish

Why don't you fucking love me?

It can also mean "what's the point?" (much like **на хуя**), or state tha[...]
point."

Хули тебе́ объясня́ть?	What's the point in explai[...]
KHOO-li tyi-BYEH ab-yi-SNYAT'	

Хули тебе́ объясня́ть.	There's no point in explaining t[...]
KHOO-li tyi-BYEH ab-yi-SNYAT'	

Some dickhead / хуй

Now we'll turn from phrases and interjections to more nouns formed from the root **хуй-**. Of course, **хуй** itself is a noun, referring to the male reproductive organ in a literal sense, in addition to the range of meanings of terms derived from it. It can also refer (synecdochically!) to a man — "some guy, some dude."

The euphemisms **хер** and **хрен** can be used in this sense — but not **фиг**.

Како́й-то хуй всё звони́т.	Some dickhead keeps calling.
ka-KOY-tuh KOOY vsyo zvah-NEET	

С днём рожде́ния, ста́рый хрен!	Happy birthday, you old fart!
ZDNYOM rah-ZHDYEH-ni-yuh, STA-ry khren!	

Though not heard too often in standard **мат** phrases, it's worth pointing out that **хуй** — like many nouns — has both a diminutive form (**хуёк**) and an augmentative form (**хуи́ще**). Note that the latter remains masculine, despite the neuter-looking ending.

Fuckery / хуйня́

Хуйня́ is one of the most common words of **мат**, combining the root **хуй-** (or any of its euphemisms) with the noun suffix **-ня** seen in a close non-**мат** equivalent: **болтовня́**, meaning "nonsense, babbling, hot air, chatter" (from the verb **болта́ть** АЙ: to babble, flap one's tongue). **Хуйня́** can mean: 1) nonsense, nonsensical or useless "stuff"; 2) nonsensical or useless speech; 3) a particular sensless, useless thing (for this meaning, see the following entry!).

One can think of several non-**мат** equivalents, like **чушь**, ерунда, or чепуха (all off which mean nonsense).

Note how the form **хрень** differs slighly in form from the others (it's an **и**-noun).

хуйня́ ➡	херня́ ➡	хрень ➡	фигня́
khooy-NYAH	kher-NYAH	KHREN'	fig-NYAH

Depending on context, these words could refer almost anything. Here are a few very simple, typical examples:

Что за хуйня?!
shto za khoo-NYAH

What the fuck is this?
What the fuck are you talking about?

Что это за хуйня лежит под столом?
shto e-tuh za khoo-NYA li-ZHEET pahd stah-LOM

What is that shit lying under the table?

— **Ты слышал? Ленин жив!**
— **Хуйня какая-то.**

"Did you hear? Lenin lives!"
"Bullshit."

— ty SLY-shul? LYEH-nin zhiv!
— khoo-NYA ka-ka-yuh-tuh

This can also mean "nothing," in a dismissive sense: no problem, no worries, etc.

— **Я разбил стакан!**
— **Хуйня!**

"I broke a class?"
"Fuck that, who gives a shit."

— ya raz-BEEL sta-KAN
— khoo-NYA

Remember: if this word isn't the subject, its ending will be changed! See box below!

Он такую хуйню говорит!
on ta-KOO-yoo khuy-NYOO guh-vah-REET

He's so full of shit! He "talks such shit."

Declining nouns...

Keep in mind that whenever you use a noun in Russian, its endings must be changed in accordance with its role in the sentence. One the one hand, this book can't possibly give examples covering noun declension in full; meanwhile, this isn't always useful, since many **мат** expressions are set phrases that are usually restricted to a single case usage.

However, *stand-alone nouns* like **хуй** and **хуйня** can certainly be used with a full range of case endings. And the nouns we've just seen include three slightly tricky declension patterns. First, **хуй** is a soft masculine noun, like **музей** or **герой** — but, unlike these, it is *end-stressed* (that is, the stress always falls on its case endings). Second, **хуйня** (and **херня**, **фигня**) is a soft feminine. Finally, **хрень** is an "**и**-noun" (also called "3rd-declension" in many textbooks).

Here are the forms; a more complete list of declension patterns is in the back of the book.

	sing.	pl.		sing.		sing.
nom.	хуй	хуи	nom.	хуйня	nom.	хрень
gen.	хуя	хуёв	gen.	хуйни	gen.	хрени
acc.	хуй	хуи	acc.	хуйню	acc.	хрень
dat.	хую	хуям	dat.	хуйне	dat.	хрени
prep.	хуе	хуях	prep.	хуйне	prep.	хрени
instr.	хуём	хуями	instr.	хуйнёй	instr.	хренью

Fuckery / хуета

Near-synonymous with **хуйня** is the less common noun **хуета**. This is another example of a **мат** noun based on an obvious non-**мат** one — in this case, **суета**, meaning "vanity" (in the sense of empty, futile behavior) or "fuss" (getting all worked up for no reason, etc.). So, **хуета** can simply fill in for **суета**, or, more commonly, refer to something useless or pointless, like **хуйня**.

Это всё хуета.   That's all much ado about nothing.
e-tuh VSYO khoo-yi-TAH.

Some fucking thingamajig / хуёвина

The noun **хуёвина** is similar to **хуйня** in its third meaning — some senseless or use-less thing. But where **хуйня** suggests "stuff" or nonsense in a more general sense, **хуёвина** is more suggestive of some (small) particular item that is puzzling in some regard: 1) some little thing whose purpose is not known; or 2) some thing whose pur-pose is known, but whose actual name (perhaps of a technical nature) is not known. In this role, it acts much like such English words as "thingamajig," "gadget," "gizmo," or "doodad."

хуёвина	херовина	хреновина	фиговина
khoo-YO-vi-nuh	kher-O-vi-nuh	khren-O-vi-nuh	fig-O-vi-nuh

This is therefore one of several **мат** expressions one may hear, perhaps surprisingly, in speech that is "technical" in nature and doesn't even necessarily involve real cursing, anger, etc. — think do-it-yourself home repairs, furniture assembly, etc.

Что это за хуёвина?   What the fuck is this little thing?
shto eh-tuh ya khoo-YO-vi-nuh

Принеси мне эту белую хуёвину.   Bring me that white whatchamacallit.
pri-nyeh-SEE mnyeh eh-too BYEH-loo-yoo khoo-YO-vi-noo

Declining nouns...

All the forms above are ordinary hard fem-inine nouns. If you compare these endings and those of the soft feminine noun хуйня on the previous page, you'll see that they're really the same endings — but the forms they assume in **хуйня** all reflect the fact that its stem ends in a soft **н**. The stem of **хуёвина** ends, of course, in a hard **н**.

	singular	plural
nom.	хуёвин**а**	хуёвин**ы**
gen.	хуёвин**ы**	хуёв**ин**
acc.	хуёвин**у**	хуёвин**ы**
dat.	хуёвин**е**	хуёвин**ам**
prep.	хуёвин**е**	хуёвин**ах**
instr.	хуёвин**ой**	хуёвин**ами**

Really fucking bad / ху<u>ё</u>вый

Now we've come to a series of extremely common *adjectives* formed from **хуй** and its euphemisms. Perhaps better than any other examples, these show how so many **мат** expressions have little if anything to do with the literal meaning of their root — first, because these adjectives from **хуй** have nothing to do with male genitalia, and, second, they can mean everything from "big" to "good" to "bad."

The first, **ху<u>ё</u>вый**, means "really fucking bad." Here are all four variations:

ху<u>ё</u>вый	хер<u>о</u>вый	хрен<u>о</u>вый	фиг<u>о</u>вый
khoo-YO-vy	kher-O-vy	khren-O-vy	fig-O-vy

Давн<u>о</u> не пил так<u>о</u>е ху<u>ё</u>вое п<u>и</u>во.
dav-NOH nye peel ta·KO-yeh khoo-YO-vuh-yeh PEE-vuh

It's been a while since I drank beer this fucking disgusting.

This can also be used adverbially (**ху<u>ё</u>во**) to express how you're feeling, how things are going, etc. — mirroring subjectless constructions such as **Мне пл<u>о</u>хо.**

— **Как ты себ<u>я</u> ч<u>у</u>вствуешь?**
— **Ху<u>ё</u>во.**

— kak ty si-BYAH CHOOST-voo-yish?
— khoo-YO-vuh

"How do you feel?"
"Like fucking shit."

ХУЙНЯ

КАКАЯ-ТО...

Declining adjectives...

Like nouns, all adjectives in Russian decline — they change their endings to reflect their role in the sentence. Adjectives must agree — in grammatical gender, number (singular or plural), and case — with the noun they modify.

Since our examples include only a few case endings, here's a full set of forms for ordinary "hard" adjectives. All the adjectives here — **хуёвый**, **охуенный**, **охуительный** — follow this pattern. The row marked "anim." shows those forms of animate nouns (people and animals) for which the *accusative* looks like the *genitive*.

	singular			plural
	masculine	**feminine**	**neuter**	**all genders**
nom.	хуёв**ый**	хуёв**ая**	хуёв**ое**	хуёв**ые**
gen.	хуёв**ого**	хуёв**ой**	хуёв**ого**	хуёв**ых**
acc.	хуёв**ый**	хуёв**ую**	хуёв**ое**	хуёв**ые**
anim.	хуёв**ого**			хуёв**ых**
dat.	хуёв**ому**	хуёв**ой**	хуёв**ому**	хуёв**ым**
prep.	хуёв**ом**	хуёв**ой**	хуёв**ом**	хуёв**ых**
instr.	хуёв**ым**	хуёв**ой**	хуёв**ым**	хуёв**ыми**

Fucking amazing, fucking huge / охуенный

The next adjective, **охуенный**, means either "huge" or "amazing," or a little bit of both. While the full set of euphemisms exists in theory, the middle two are rare.

охуенный	охеренный	охренённый	офигенный
ah-khoo-YEN-ny	ah-kher-YEN-ny	ah-khren-YEN-ny	ah-fig-YEN-ny

Собака у него просто охуенная.   His dog is fucking huge (amazing).
sah-BAH-kuh oo nyi-VO PRO-stuh ah-khoo-YEN-nuh-yuh

This too can be used in subjectless constructions, like **Мне плохо**.

— **Как ты себя чувствуешь?**   "How do you feel?"
— **Охуенно!**   "Fucking great!"

— kak ty si-BYAH CHOOST-voo-yish?
— ah-khoo-YEN-nuh

Fucking fantastic / охуительный

Our final adjective from **хуй** means "great, amazing, incredible." Once again, the middle two euphemisms are rarely heard.

охуи́тельный	➡	охери́тельный	➡	охрени́тельный	➡	офиги́тельный
ah-khoo-EE-tyil'-ny		ah-kher-EE-tyil'-ny		ah-khren-EE-tyil'-ny		ah-fig-EE-tyil'-ny

У них пи́во охуи́тельное.
oo NEEKH PEE-vuh ah-khoo-EE-tyil'-nuh-yeh

Their beer is fucking outstanding.

This too can be used in subjectless constructions, like **Мне пло́хо**.

— Как ты себя́ чу́вствуешь?
— Охуи́тельно!

"How do you feel?"
"Fucking great!"

— kak ty si-BYAH CHOOST-voo-yish?
— ah-khoo-YEE-tyil'-nuh

Creating adverbs from adjectives...

We can form adverbs from most hard adjectives in Russian by replacing the long adjectival endings we just reviewed (**-ый**, **-ая**, **-ое**, **-ые**) with the ending **-о**. Adverbs have *only one form*; since they typically modify verbs — not nouns — they don't change gender, case, or number for purposes of agreement. These adverbs — and adjectives that look just like them — are used in a number of very simple, very common constructions.

Here are examples of all three of our adjectives used as adverbs, modifying verbs:

Кома́нда так хуёво игра́ет!
kah-MAHN-duh tak khoo-YO-vuh ee-GRA-yit

The team is playing like such shit!

Твой друг охуе́нно танцу́ет.
tfoy droog ah-khoo-YEN-nuh tan-TSOO-yit

Your friend is a hell of a dancer.

Ты охуи́тельно гото́вишь.
ty ah-khoo-EE-tyil'-nuh gah-TO-vish

You're a fucking great cook.

Note that these adverbs (in **-о**) are identical to short-form neuter adjectives. Here's an examples of such an adjective modifying **всё** (everything).

Всё у меня́ охуи́тельно!
vsyo oo mi-NYAH ah-khoo-EE-tyil'-nuh

Everything's fucking great with me.

Though it matters little, the forms in **-о** in such subjectless constructions as "**мне хорошо́**" are actually *adverbs*, used in subjectless constructions, used with the dative case. These are used all the time to tell how one feels, how things are going, etc.

Хуёво мне!
khoo-YO-vuh mnyeh

I feel like shit. My life fucking sucks.

Such adverbs are also used in one-word sentences to tell how things are:

Охуи́тельно!
ah-khoo-EE-tyil'-nuh

Great! That's great! Things are great!

To be out of one's fucking mind / охуеть

Now for some verbs derived from **хуй**. The first, **охуеть** ЕЙ, essentially means "to lose one's mind" — in one of three senses: 1) to be stunned, amazed, speechless, etc.; 2) to lose all shame, overstep one's bounds; or 3) to feel like total shit.

This extremely common verb comes in all four variants:

охуеть ЕЙ	охереть ЕЙ	охренеть ЕЙ	офигеть ЕЙ
ah-khoo-YET'	ah-kher-YET'	ah-khren-YET'	ah-fig-YET'

These **perfective** forms are by far the more common — used to describe any single completed act of losing one's fucking mind, as in: "When he heard the news he lost his fucking mind," or "He'll lose his fucking mind."

But, like most any Russian verb, these too come in aspectual pairs. The (derived) imperfective for **охуеть** ЕЙ is **охуевать** АЙ. Only the imperfective can be used in the present tense: "I'm losing my fucking mind." In the past, it can also describe being in the process of losing one's fucking mind, or doing so repeatedly!

Regarding conjugation patterns, the perfectives of these verbs follow what we're calling the ЕЙ pattern, while the imperfecives follow the extremely common АЙ pattern.

охуева́ть АЙ	➡	охерева́ть АЙ	➡	охренева́ть АЙ	➡	офигева́ть АЙ
ah-khoo-yeh-VAT'		ah-kher-yeh-VAT'		ah-khren-yeh-VAT'		ah-fig-yeh-VAT'

Now we have four complete aspectual pairs — and this is the form in which you should try to learn every Russian verb you encounter!

охуева́ть АЙ / охуе́ть ЕЙ	охерева́ть АЙ / охере́ть ЕЙ
охренева́ть АЙ / охрене́ть ЕЙ	офигева́ть АЙ / офиге́ть ЕЙ

Here's a full set of forms for the pair **охуева́ть** АЙ / **охуе́ть** ЕЙ. All the euphemistic pairs follow precisely the same pattern.

охуева́ть АЙ: to lose it (imperfective)		охуе́ть ЕЙ: to lose it (perfective)	
охуева́ю	I'm fucking losing it	охуе́ю	I'll fucking lose it
охуева́ешь	you're fucking losing it	охуе́ешь	you'll fucking lose it
охуева́ет	he, she's losing it	охуе́ет	he, she'll fucking lose it
охуева́ем	we're fucking losing it	охуе́ем	we'll fucking lose it
охуева́ете	you're fucking losing it	охуе́ете	you'll fuckinig lose it
охуева́ют	they're fucking losing it	охуе́ют	they'll fucking lose it
охуева́й!	lose your fucking mind!	охуе́й!	fucking lose it!
охуева́л	he was fucking losing it	охуе́л	he fucking lost it
охуева́ла	she was fucking losing it	охуе́ла	she fucking lost it
охуева́ли	they were fucking losing it	охуе́ли	they fucking lost it

One more note on these aspectual pairs... though we risk getting into too much detail, this is actually a fairly important point! Advanced students will notice that **охуе́ть** is a prefixed verb (with **о-**); this tells us that the basic underlying imperfective verb to which the **о-** was added was **хуе́ть** ЕЙ. So, in addition to the "derived" imperfectives in **о-** that we gave above, you may hear more basic, unprefixed forms like **хуе́ть**. Thus, as sometimes happens, we have "competing" aspectual pairs.

хуе́ть ЕЙ / охуе́ть ЕЙ	хере́ть ЕЙ / охере́ть ЕЙ
хрене́ть ЕЙ / охрене́ть ЕЙ	фиге́ть ЕЙ / офиге́ть ЕЙ

Here are several examples of this verb in action:

Я пр<u>о</u>сто ху<u>е</u>ю. = **Я пр<u>о</u>сто охуева<u>ю</u>.**   I'm out of my fucking mind.
ya PRO-stuh khoo-YE-yoo = ya PRO-stuh ah-khoo-yi-VA-yoo

Он охуев<u>а</u>л.   He was losing his fucking mind.
on ah-khoo-yi-VAL

Он оху<u>е</u>л.   He lost his fucking mind.
on ah-khoo-YEL

Он оху<u>е</u>ет, когд<u>а</u> узн<u>а</u>ет.   He'll lose his mind when he finds out.
on ah-khoo-YE-yit kag-DA oo-ZNA-yit

Keep in mind that this verb has three distinct meanings. First: to be surprised or amazed:

Когд<u>а</u> я сказ<u>а</u>л жен<u>е</u>, что мы   When I told my wife we'd won the
в<u>ы</u>играли в лотер<u>е</u>ю, он<u>а</u> оху<u>е</u>ла. lottery, she fucking lost it.
kag-DA ya ska-ZAL zhi-NYEH, shto my
VY-i-gra-li v lah-ti-RYEH-yoo, ah-NA ah-khoo-YE-luh

Second: to lose all shame.

— **Я в<u>ы</u>пил всю в<u>о</u>дку.**   — I drank all the vodka.
— **Ты оху<u>е</u>л!**   — Have you lost your fucking mind?
ya VY-pil fsyoo VOT-koo
ty ah-khoo-YEL

Third (and least common): to feel like total shit, to "be dying."

Мы оху<u>е</u>ли от х<u>о</u>лода.   — We froze our fucking asses off.
my ah-khoo-YEL-i aht KHO-luh-duh

Finally, the perfective infinitive can be used all by itself, as a simple interjection.

Оху<u>е</u>ть!   Fucking wow! Are you fucking kidding?
ah-khoo-YET'

Or, with **можно** (it is possible...), also expressing incredulity:

Оху<u>е</u>ть м<u>о</u>жно!   It's enough to make you lose your mind.
ah-khoo-YET' MOZH-nuh

To work one's fucking ass off / ху<u>я</u>чить

The verb **ху<u>я</u>чить** is essentially the **мат** equivalent for **раб<u>о</u>тать** (to work) — but, as one might guess, it implies a negative attitude toward "fucking" work, and suggest prolonged, tedious, soul-crushing toil of one kind or another. Since it describes an ongoing activity, it — like **раб<u>о</u>тать** itself — doesn't come in an aspectual pair, unless we count the somewhat special perfective form **поху<u>я</u>чить** (like пораб<u>о</u>тать), which means "to work for a bit" (one can add the prefix **по-** to almost any imperfective "activity" verb to create a perfective verb meaning "to do the activity for a bit").

To be a bit more specific, **хуячить** describes doing ("dicking") something over and over (tediously), or with a great expenditure of energy — striking, swinging, digging, shooting, drinking — almost anything, depending on the context. Here's a nice example from the band **Ленинград**, who rose to fame in the early 2000's thanks in large part to their unabashed use of **мат** in their lyrics:

Вот будет лето —	vot BOO-dyit LYEH-tuh	When summer comes
поедем на дачу;	pah-YEH-dyim na DAH-choo	We'll go to the dacha,
В руки лопату —	v ROO-ki lah-PAH-too	Grab a shovel, and
хуячим, хуячим!	khoo-YAH-chim, khoo-YAH-chim	Shovel our asses off.

That's from the title track off their classic 2000 album **Дачники** (Dacha-goers). Any aficionado of Russian **мат** can't afford to miss Leningrad; after going through this introductory course, you can embark on advanced studies with these masters of **мат**, and truly appreciate their lyrics!

We can clearly visualize the action being described — the shovel going up and down, up and down, "whacking" over and over again into the dirt.

ХУЯЧИТЬ, ХУЯЧИТЬ И ХУЯЧИТЬ!

Here are several examples of this verb in action. It can mean almost anything:

Приехал на дачу и начал хуячить.   He arrived at the dacha and got to work.
pri-YEH-khul na DA-choo i NA-cha-l khoo-YA-chit'

Он уже третий день водку хуячит.   He's been drinking vodka for three days.
on oo-ZHE TRE-ti dyen' VOT-koo khoo-YA-chit

Хватит тебе хуячить молотком!   Enough with the fucking hammering!
KHVA-tit ti-BYE khoo-YA-chit' muh-laht-KOM

Дождь всё хуячит и хуячит.   The rain refuses to fucking stop.
dosht' vsyo khoo-YA-chit ee khoo-YA-chit

To give a good fucking whack / хуя́кнуть

This brings us to a second set of verbs that describe not working in general (doing the same thing over and over as a prolonged process), but rather discreet acts of whacking (literally, "dicking") something. Though these do come in pairs, the perfective forms are the most common and most useful. In a practical sense, they can even be thought of as the perfective counterparts of verbs like **хуячить**, though they don't actually form an apectual pair. The perfective forms are:

хуякнуть НУ ➡ херакнуть НУ ➡ хренакнуть НУ ➡ фигакнуть НУ

khoo-YAK-noot'   kher-AK-noot'   khren-AK-noot'   fig-AK-noot'

These perfectives are **semelfactives** — perfective forms that emphasize doing something **once**. They follow the НУ conjugation pattern, which is typical of semelfactives; to take some everyday examples: **кашлять** АЙ means "to be coughing," while **кашлянуть** НУ means "to cough once," to "give a cough." Or, **дёргать** АЙ means to "be tugging or jerking on something," while **дёрнуть** НУ means to "give something a tug." Verbs like **хуякнуть** НУ are a great example: they mean to strike something *once*, to "give something a whack." We'll see other **мат** semelfactives later.

The true imperfectives for these verbs are АЙ verbs. Here are the pairs:

хуякать АЙ / хуякнуть НУ	херакать АЙ / херакнуть НУ
хренакать АЙ / хренакнуть НУ	фигакать АЙ / фигакнуть НУ

Like **хуячить**, these verbs can mean all kinds of things, depending on context, but the general idea is to "strike a blow," to "whack."

Я взял бутылку и хуякнул его по голове.   I took a bottle and whacked him
ya vzyal boo-TYL-koo i khoo-YAK-nool yi-VO pah guh-lah-VYE   in the head with it.

Here are the patterns for the И and НУ verbs we've just seen:

хуячить И: to work (imperfective)	
хуя́чу	I fucking work
хуя́чишь	you fucking work
хуя́чит	he / she fucking works
хуя́чим	we fucking work
хуя́чите	you fucking work
хуя́чат	they fucking work
хуя́чь!	fucking work!
хуя́чил	he fucking worked
хуя́чила	she fucking worked
хуя́чили	they fucking worked

хуякнуть НУ: to whack (perfective)	
хуя́кну	I'll whack
хуя́кнешь	you'll whack
хуя́кнет	he, she'll whack
хуя́кнем	we'll whack
хуя́кнете	you'll whack
хуя́кнут	they'll whack
хуя́кни!	whack!
хуя́кнул	he whacked
хуя́кнула	she whacked
хуя́кнули	they whacked

Bang! / хуя́к

The form **хуя́к** — which doesn't decline — can be used in narratives to represent the sound that results from the verb **хуякнуть** — the sound of a "whack" (of whatever kind). Think English words such as "Bang!" "Bam!" or "Wham!" This is the equivalent of the non-**мат** "**Бац**!"

Он схватил молото́к, и — хуя́к!   He grabbed the hammer, and... bam!
on skhvah-TEEL muh-lah-TOK ee khoo-YAK

At the start of the previous chapter, we noted that **хуй** is probably the first single word that would likely come to mind when people think of **мат**. In terms of entire **мат** phrases, "**Пошёл на хуй!**" ("Fuck you!" — literally, "Go onto a cock!") comes immediately to mind. But competing with it for primacy is the phrase "**Ёб твою мать!**" We could loosely translate this too as "Fuck you!" — but its literal meaning is much less clear, as we'll see in a moment...

One thing that's immediately clear is that the phrase involves a form of the verb **ебать**, meaning "to fuck," combined with "your mother" — as the direct object! The verb **ебать** is built from our next root, the root for "fucking" — **ёб** (or, in unstressed positions, **еб** — remember, the "ё" can only occur in a stressed syllable).

So, this chapter will explore all common words and expressions built from the root **ёб**.

Fuck you! / Ёб твою мать!

We (or at least, some of us) say and hear the English phrase "Fuck you!" so often that we likely have never really paused to think about what it means. Of course, we all get the basic point — but the literal, grammatical meaning is somewhat unclear. It doesn't quite make sense as an imperative (like "Go fuck yourself!"). Yet, if we read it as a conjugated verb, then what's the subject? Does it mean "I fuck you?" Does it propose that you be fucked by someone — anyone — else, as in "May someone fuck you?"

Luckily, we don't need to resolve this debate — I only mention it to illustrate a similar ambiguity in the near-ubiquitous **мат** phrase "**Ёб твою мать!**" Like the English "Fuck you," it is used so often that few Russians have likely wondered what it *literally* means. The "**твою мать**" part is obvious — "your mother" in the accusative. But the form of **ебать** — "**ёб**" — is *not* an imperative (that would be "**еби!**"). It is in fact a masculine past-tense form, as in "he fucked," or "I (male speaker) fucked," or "you (a male) fucked"... your mother.

It seems that none of these interpretations is correct. Believe it or not, the consensus among linguists seems to be that the historical subject of the verb **ёб** — now lost — is **пёс** (a male dog); furthermore, the form **ёб** is neither an imperative nor past tense, but a subjunctive form with **чтобы** (may...). The full original phrase was something like "**Чтобы пёс ёб твою мать**" (May a dog fuck your mother).

But wait, there's more! It is speculated that this was not originally a curse or insult directed at the interlocutor's biological mother, but rather a kind of oath, like the English "May lightning strike me if... (that is, if I'm not speaking the truth)." And the "mother" here is Mother Earth, from the days of the pagan cult of "**мать сыра земля**" (the "damp mother earth").

In practice, none of this really matters; in terms of usage, the phrase "**Ёб твою мать!**" is the equivalent of the English "Fuck you!" In this sense, it's a go-to insult, on par with "**Пошёл на хуй!**"

Ёб твою мать!   Fuck you!
YOP tvah-YOO mat'

To fuck / ебать

The verb **ебать** itself simply means 1) "to fuck," in a very literal sense; 2) to "fuck with" in a more figurative sense — for example, in the phrase **ебать мозг** (to fuck someone's brain, used with the dative); 3) to fuck someone up, beat up. This is an imperfective verb, describing "fucking" as an activity, an ongoing process — or as a repeated or habitual activity. Its perfective, **выебать**, describes the activity as a completed, one-time act — as in, to give someone a good fucking (or a good beating).

A non-**мат** (but still quite vulgar) equivalent is the aspectual pair **трахать** АЙ / **трахнуть** НУ — something like the English "to bang."

Here are some simple examples:

Ёб твою мать!   Fuck you!
YOP tvah-YOO mat'

Говорят, он ебёт подругу своей жены!   They say he's fucking his wife's friend!
guh-vahr-YAT on yi-BYOT pah-DROO-goo svah-YEY zhe-NY

Он выебал подругу своей жены.   He fucked his wife's friend.
on VY-yi-bal pah-DROO-goo svah-YEY zye-NY

Я тебя выебу.   I'm gonna fuck you up good.
ya ti-BYAH VY-yi-boo

Не ебёт.   Who fucking cares.
nye yi-BYOT

Не еби мне мозги.   Don't fuck my brains.
nye yi-BEE mnyeh mahz-GEE   (compare: трахать мозги)

The infinitive can be used as a simple interjection, expressing surprise or amazement:

Ебать!   Wow. Fucking unbelievable.
yi-BAT'

The conjugation of **ебать** is irregular. Pay particular attention to the past-tense forms, where irregular and regular forms compete. Here's the aspectual pair:

ебать: to fuck (imperfective)		**выебать**: to fuck (perfective)	
ебу	I fuck	выебу	I'll fuck
ебёшь	you fuck	выебешь	you'll fuck
ебёт	he / she fucks	выебет	he, she'll fuck
ебём	we fuck	выебем	we'll fuck
ебёте	you fuck	выебете	you'll fuck
ебут	they fuck	выебут	they'll fuck
еби!	fuck!	выеби!	fuck!
ёб (ебал)	he was fucking	выеб (выебал)	he fucked
ебла (ебала)	she was fucking	выебла (выебала)	she fucked
ебли (ебали)	they were fucking	выебли (выебали)	they fucked

To fuck each other; to get fucked / ебаться

If we add the reflexive particle **-ся** (or, after a final vowel, **-сь**) to the verb **ебать**, we get the reflexive verb **ебаться**. Reflexive verbs generally have three basic meanings: 1) true **reflexivity** (to "x" oneself); 2) **passivity** (to be "x-ed" or to get "x-ed"); and 3) **reciprocity** (to "x" each other). A fourth — spontaneity — is much less common.

The verb **ебаться** is a nice example of how not every reflexive verb is necessarily used in all three senses. For example: **одевать** means "to dress (someone)," while **одеваться** can be understood to mean "to be dressed" (passive) or "to dress one-self" (reflexive), but it isn't used in a reciprocal sense (to dress each other). Meanwhile, **ебаться** can be understood passively ("to get fucked") or reciprocally ("to fuck each other"), but — note well! — not reflexively, ("to fuck oneself). This reminds us that in **мат** — as in all language study — we have to resist translating a given idiom literally and the result to necessarily "work." Russians simply don't say "**Ебись!**" in the sense that English speakers use "Go fuck yourself!" This simply is not a Russian "idiom." However, we'll see that the form "**ебись**" is used in other senses.

Here's a *reciprocal* usage (to fuck each other):

Они ебутся, или нет? ah-NEE yi-BOO-tsa ili nyet	Are they fucking (each other) or not?

Here are several examples of a saying, with various pronouns, that can be understood passively, i.e. "May you be fucked..."

(Да) ебись оно конём! da yi-BEES' ah-NO kah-NYOM	"Let it get fucked by a horse (конь)."
(Да) ебись она конём! da yi-BEES' ah-NAH kah-NYOM	"She can get fucked by a horse."
(Да) ебись ты конём! da yi-BEES' ty kah-NYOM	"May you be fucked by a horse."
(Да) ебись оно всё конём! da yi-BEES' ah-NO vsyo kah-NYOM	"Let it get all get fucked by a horse."

To fucking annoy the hell out of / заебать

Now let's look at some prefixed forms of **ебать**. Adding prefixes produces new "fucking-related" verbs that have new meanings — and, as so often happens with **мат**, these need not always be understood literally. Let's start with the prefix **за-**, one meaning of which is "to do something to excess," to the point of overkill or exhaustion. When we add this to **ебать**, the result is a *perfective* verb: **заебать**: to fuck (someone) to the point of exhaustion, to "fuck them silly." Its derived imperfective, **заёбывать**, conjugates according to the АЙ pattern.

заёбывать АЙ: to fucking annoy (imperf.)		**заебать**: to fucking annoy (perf.)	
заёбываю	I fucking annoy	заебу	I'll fucking annoy
заёбываешь	you fucking annoy	заебёшь	you'll fucking annoy
заёбывает	he, she fucking annoys	заебёт	he, she'll fucking annoy
заёбываем	we fucking annoy	заебём	we'll fucking annoy
заёбываете	you fucking annoy	заебёте	you'll fucking annoy
заёбывают	they fucking annoy	заебут	they'll fucking annoy
заёбывай!	fucking annoy!	заеби!	fucking annoy!
заёбывал	he was fucking annoying	заебал	he fucking annoyed
заёбывала	she was fucking annoying	заебала	she fucking annoyed
заёбывали	they were fucking annoying	заебали	they fucking annoyed

Again, this verb could be used literally in the sense of some vigorous sexual act, but it is used most often in the sense of "driving someone fucking crazy." In this meaning, a close non-**мат** equivalent is **надоедать** АЙ / **надоесть**: to annoy (the latter conjugates like **есть** (to eat): надоеду, надоедешь; надоел, надоело, etc). Whereas **надоесть** takes a *dative* object ("**Ты мне надоел!**"), **заебать** takes the *accusative* — literally, you have "fucked me to excess!" For example:

Ты меня заебал!
ty mi-NYA za-yi-BAL

I'm fucking sick of you!
(said to a man)

Ты меня заебала!
ty mi-NYA za-yi-BAL-uh

I'm fucking sick of you!
(said to a woman)

Всё заебало!
fsyo za-yi-BA-luh

I'm fucking sick of everything!

Как вы все заебали!
kak vy fsyeh za-yi-BA-li

I'm so fucking sick of all of you!

Ты всех заебал!
ty fsyekh za-yi-BAL

Everyone's fucking sick of you.
(said to a man)

Он меня заёбывает иногда.
on mi-NYA za-YO-by-vuh-yit ee-nahg-DA

He gets on my fucking nerves sometime

Oddly enough, the perfective imperative form "**Заебись!**" has the very common meaning of "Fucking fantastic!" or "Wow!" It can be used all alone as an interjection.

(Всё) заебись!
(fsyo) za-yi-BEES'

(Everything's) fucking great!

Всё было заебись.   Everything was fucking great.
fsyo BY-luh za-yi-BEES'

To fuck someone over / наебать

If we add a different prefix (**на**-), we get a new "**ебать**" verb: **наебать**, which means "to fuck (someone) over" — to trick, mislead, etc. Its basic non-**мат** equivalent would be **обманывать** АЙ / **обмануть** НУ^{shift} (to trick, deceive).

Again, we derive an imperfective (**наёбывать**) to complete our aspectual pair. It's now obvious that our "base" pair for prefixed "fucking" verbs is -**ёбывать** АЙ / -**ебать**; we already have two prefixed verbs from this "family" of verbs:

заёбывать АЙ / заебать	наёбывать АЙ / наебать
to fucking annoy the hell out of	to fuck over, trick, deceive

If we add a different prefix (**на**-), we get a new "ебать" verb: **наебать**, which means "to fuck (someone) over" — to trick, mislead, etc. Its basic non-**мат** equivalent would be **обманывать** АЙ / **обмануть** НУ (to trick, deceive).

Again, we derive an imperfective (**наёбывать**) to complete our aspectual pair. It's now obvious that our "base" pair for prefixed "fucking" verbs is -**ёбывать** АЙ / -**ебать**; we already have two prefixed verbs from this family of verbs:

Меня на работе наебали.   I got fucked over at work.
mi-NYA na ra-BO-tyeh na-yi-BA-li

Меня не наебать.   You can't fucking fool me.
mi-NYA nye na-yi-BAT'

Он всех наёбывает.   He's screwing everyone over.
on fsyekh na-YO-by-vuh-yit

For a great example of **мат** in action, check out the song **Наебали** (originally by a band called **Хуй забей**, and memorably covered by the venerable Russian rock icon Boris Grebenshchikov). It is sung from the point of view of two soldiers abandoned and left to die ("fucked over") by their supposed comrades. It begins like this:

Жаль подмога	ZHAL' pad-MO-guh	Too bad, help
не пришла —	nye pri-SHLA	didn't come,
Подкрепление	puhd-kryi-PLYE-ni-yeh	Reinforcements
не прислали.	nye pri-SLA-li	weren't sent.
Нас осталось	nas ah-STAH-luhs'	Just the two
только два —	TOL'-kuh DVA	of us remain;
Нас с тобою	nas s tah-BO-yoo	They
Наебали.	na-yi-BA-li	fucked us over.

To fucking leave / съеб<u>а</u>ть

Let's add another (less common) **еб<u>а</u>ть** verb, with the prefix "**с**." It is the equivalent of **сбег<u>а</u>ть** АЙ / **сбеж<u>а</u>ть** — to run off. Since this "**с**" is a hard consonant, we need to add a hard sign (**ъ**) here to show that it remains hard despite being followed by the soft vowel "**е**." This verb can also be used with the reflexive particle, with much the same meaning, but in some cases with the idea of hiding or finding cover (the equivalent of **скрыв<u>а</u>ться** АЙ / **скр<u>ы</u>ться** ОЙ^{stem}). Here are both aspectual pairs:

съёбывать АЙ / съеб<u>а</u>ть	съёбываться АЙ / съеб<u>а</u>ться
to fucking leave	to fucking leave (escape, hide)

In fact, the song we just sampled includes this verb as well:

Нам от см<u>е</u>рти не съеб<u>а</u>тся! nam aht SMYER-ti nye syi-BAH-tsa	We can't fucking escape death!
Съеб<u>и</u> отс<u>ю</u>да! syi-BEE aht-SYOO-duh	Get the fuck outta here!
Мне н<u>а</u>до съеб<u>а</u>ть отс<u>ю</u>да. mnyeh NA-duh syi-BAT' aht-SYOO-duh	I've got to get the fuck outta here.

To fucking lose, waste / проеб<u>а</u>ть

A final prefixed form involves **про**- (through, past) — here in the sense of "missing" or letting slip by. As we've seen in multiple examples, many **мат** verbs can mean almost anything, depending on context; with this verb, the general idea is losing or letting something go to waste — "fucking something up."

проёбывать АЙ / проеб<u>а</u>ть
to fucking lose, waste, miss

Он все сво<u>и</u> д<u>е</u>ньги проеб<u>а</u>л. on fsvyeh sva-EE DYEN'-gi pra-yi-BAL	He pissed away all his money.
Мы всё проеб<u>а</u>ли. my vsyo pra-yi-BAH-li	We fucked everything up.

To give a quick fuck / ебан<u>у</u>ть

Finally, we have a perfective semelfactive — unprefixed — meaning simply "to fuck once," or "to give a quick fuck": **ебан<u>у</u>ть**. Like most semelfactives, it follows the **НУ** pattern. It can be used in a literal, sexual sense, but more often it would suggest any sort of quick, one-time action — striking a blow, throwing down a drink, stealing something, or doing something quickly. This is essentially a **ёб**-derived synonym for the **хуй**-derived semelfactive we saw earlier (**хуякнуть**).

Хочешь пивка ебануть?   Wanna grab a fucking beer?
KHO-chish pif-KAH yi-bah-NOOT'

Кто-то ебанул меня по голове.   Someone whacked me on the head.
KTO-tuh yi-ba-NOOL mi-NYAH pah guh-lah-VYEH

The *past passive participle* (PPP) of this verb — **ебанутый** (literally, "fucked") — can mean "batshit crazy," "fucked in the head." For example:

Они совсем ебанутые.   They're completely fucking batshit.
ah-NEE saf-SYEM yi-ba-NOO-ty-yeh

This brings us to the reflexive form of the verb — **ебануться** НУ, which can mean to go insane, "to lose one's fucking mind."

Ты ебанулся, что ли?   Have you lost your fucking mind?
ty yi-ba-NOOL-sya, shto li

Ебануться можно.   It's enough to make you lose your mind.
yi-ba-NOO-tsa MOZH-nuh

It can also work as a passive form of **ебануть** (to strike), meaning "to be struck" — i.e. to hit one's head, bump into something, etc.

Я ебанулся головой об потолок.   I fucking hit my head on the ceiling.
ya yi-ba-NOOL-sya guh-lah-VOY ahb puh-tah-LOK

Fucking around / ебля

Now let's turn to a few common nouns built from the root **ёб**-. The first, **ебля**, is the simple noun equivalent of the verb **ебать** (to fuck), meaning "fucking" (literally) and something like the English "fucking around," in the sene of a tiring, irritating activity.

Я устал от всей этой ебли.   I'm tired of all this fucking around.
ya oo-STAL aht fsyey e-tuhy YEB-li

A fucking face, mouth / ебало

The noun **ебало**, is roughly equivalent to "fucking face." It is the **мат** equivalent of such words as **рожа**, **рыло** or **харя**, each suggestive of an ugly "mug" or animal's snout (instead of a human face). These words too — all rather crude — are commonly used in **мат**, though they are not themselves **мат**. We can tell someone to "close" their **ебало** — as in the English "Shut your fucking mouth!"

Закр<u>о</u>й еб<u>а</u>ло! (or: заткн<u>и</u>, завал<u>и</u> еб<u>а</u>ло!)   Shut your fucking mouth!
ya-KROY yi-BA-luh

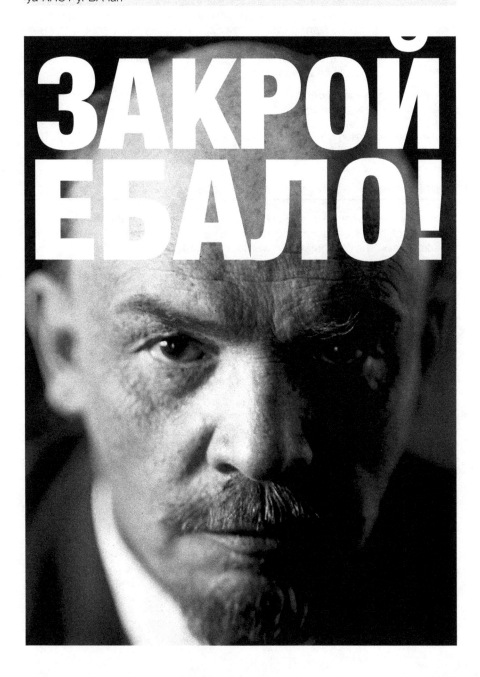

A fucking dumbass / долбоёб

This fairly common insult suggests someone who fucks constantly (the verb **долбить** means to strike or say something over and over again. Loosely, we might say that a **долбоёб** is constantly fucking people's brains (or, fucking things up) with his stupidity. As we'd usually expect, this grammatically masculine noun refers to a *male* dumbass; the female version would be **долбоёбка**.

Почему ты такой долбоёб?   Why are you suck a fucking dumbass?
puh-chi-MOO ty tah-KOY duhl-bah-YOP

Another good -**ёб** insult is **уёбок** — a fucker (a misbegotten product of fucking). The related augmentative **уёбище** can also refer to some *thing* that's really fucked up.

A fucking joke / наёб (наёбка, наебалово)

Most Russian verbs have a corresponding noun of one kind or another that names the activity of the verb, or its result. For prefixed verbs, the noun would always involve the same prefix. The noun **наёб** (or **наёбка**, or **наебалово**) for example, is the noun version of the verb **наёбывать** АЙ / **наебать** (to trick, deceive), which we already saw. So **наёбка** means something like "trickery, deceit" or "a trick, a prank, a joke (played on someone)," etc. Its non-**мат** equivalent would likely be **обман** (deceit).

Это наёб.   It's a fucking scam.
e-tuh na-YOB

Fucking untranslatable? / изъёб

Admittedly, this isn't an exhaustive dictionary of **мат** — just an introduction. So we aren't giving every last **мат** expression, just the basics. But it's worth giving a some-what more obscure expression to give a sense of what's out there. As you encounter new **мат** expressions, you may realize that 1) the meaning is often only clear from a concrete context, and 2) even then, it may be very hard to translate with one or two English words (even if we throw in a "fucking" for good measure).

For example, an **изъёб** is a needlessly complicated solution to what should be a sim-ple problem. Maybe we could speak of someone "fucking themselves into knots" in their attempt to get something done. I can share a personal anecdote about the first time I heard this term: a friend and I were being driven in a taxi through the middle of Moscow when the driver pulled onto what seemed like a simple off-ramp, which then proceeded to wind back and forth, and seemingly in circles, before finally joining up with another highway — leaving us completely disoriented. My friend, never at a loss for words, called the whole thing an **изъёб** on the part of the highway engineers.

Что за изъёб!   "What a fucking needlessly complicated solution
shto za iz-YOP   to what should be a simple problem!"

This context was so clear that I felt I'd understood immediately what he meant, but of course I asked for confirmation. When you hear new words with these now-familiar **мат** roots, don't hesitate to ask for an explanation — if Russians are using **мат** in the first place, they'll likely be delighted at the opportunity to explain it a foreigner!

Also, try analyzing the word to get some idea of its literal meaning. Since the meaning of the **мат** root itself is usually clear, this often involves looking at prefixes and suffixes. If it's a noun, you may able to associate it with a verb. In this case, **изъёб** is related to the perfective verb **изъебать**, a rough equivalent of "fucking the hell out of" someone in English, or "fucking every which way." Adding a reflexive particle gives **изъеб<u>а</u>ться** — literally, to "fuck the hell out of yourself" or "be fucked to the point of exhaustion" or perhaps to "fuck one's way into knots" in the overzealous pursuit of some goal. But capturing this in translation is no easy task. Always keep in mind that the "literal" meaning of a term may ultimately be hard to nail down — in which case, don't insist on getting to the bottom of it; just try to understand the expression's general sense, and how it's used — and this is where concrete situations are particularly helpful. This general approach should be taken with any Russian word — not only with **мат**.

Always remember: **мат** uses the very same word-building principles and elements (prefixes, suffixes, verb types, etc.) as ordinary Russian words! The only difference is that its the roots it uses to build words are inherently obscene!

Fucking, fucked / <u>ё</u>банный

Quite often, the only way to give a sense of **мат**'s obscenity in English translation is to sprinkle the word "fucking" everywhere. The actual **мат** word closest to the English "fucking" in terms of meaning and usage is **ёбанный** — the past perfect participle ("PPP") of **еб<u>а</u>ть**. So, **ёбанный** literally means "fucked," but it's attached to nouns in the way "fucking" is in English. Note the alternate spelling **ёбаный**.

Here's a common insult in which the PPP is used rather literally — "fucked." It can be used descriptively, i.e. "You fucked-in-the mouth so-and-so," or as an interjection:

Ёбанный в рот! YO-buh-ny v rot	Fucking hell! What the fuck!? (masculine ending)
Ёбанная в рот! YO-buh-nuh-yuh v rot	Fucking bitch! (feminine ending)

Here are examples of **<u>ё</u>банный** being used as a simple adjective, like "fucking."

Ёбанный прид<u>у</u>рок! YO-buh-ny pri-DOO-ruhk	Fucking idiot!
Где ёбанные деньги, Леб<u>о</u>вски? gdyeh YO-buh-ny-yeh DYEN'-gi li-BOF-ski	Where's the fucking money, Lebowski?

We've now come to what must be — easily — the most frequently used word in **мат**: **блядь**. It's sometimes spelled **блять**, reflecting the devoicing of the final soft "d" to a soft "t" — or, with even more comic emphasis, as **блеать** (compare such English spellings as "biyatch"). The word is said so often that it even has a shortened version: **бля**. Hearing this word — repeatedly — is a clear indication that you're hearing **мат**.

Fucking bitch / блядь (as a noun)

The literal meaning of **блядь** is "bitch." And **блядь** can certainly be used in this sense. For example:

Она такая блядь!   She's such a bitch!
ah-NA ta-KA-yuh blyat'

Не стану разговаривать с этой блядью.   I'm not about to talk to that bitch.
nye STA-noo raz-guh-VAH-ri-vuht' s E-tuhy BLYAD'-yoo

We should note that **блядь** is related to the root **блуд**, which describes moral depravity (especially sexual debauchery); that is, it does not have the literal meaning of "female dog" (as the English "bitch" does). The Russian term for "female dog" (**сука**) is also used as an insult — often in combination with **мат**! — although it itself is not considered **мат**. We'll consider this and other such words later in the book.

Он<u>а</u> так<u>ая</u> с<u>у</u>ка!
ah-NA ta-KA-yuh SOO-kuh

She's such a bitch!

Declining блядь...

When used (relatively rarely!) in its literal meaning, as a noun, **блядь** follows the feminine "**и**-noun" pattern.

Note an important stress pattern among **и**-nouns: in the *plural*, if the stress jumps to the gen. pl. ending -**ей** (as it often does, especially with monosyllabic nouns), then the dative, prepositional, and instrumental plural endings will also be stressed.

	sing.	pl.
nom.	бл**я**дь	бляд**и**
gen.	бляд**и**	бляд**ей**
acc.	бл**я**дь	бляд**и**
dat.	бляд**и**	бляд**ям**
prep.	бляд**и**	бляд**ях**
instr.	бляд**ью**	бляд**ями**

Fuck! / блядь (as interjection)

Statistically, however, **блядь** is rarely used in its literal sense. First, it can be a simple interjection — "**Блядь!**" — expressing surprise, anger, frustration, etc. It's probably the first word that comes to mind when you, say, drop something or stub your toe.

Блядь!
blyat'

Fuck! Shit! Goddammit!
(said after dropping something, for example)

Блядь, я в<u>о</u>дку заб<u>ы</u>л!
blyat', ya VOT-koo za-BYL

Fuck, I forgot the vodka!

Here we come to another extremely common euphemism: "**Блин!**" Literally — "Pancake!" Again, note the phonetic similarity to **блядь** — much as we saw with **хер** and **хрен** with regard to **хуй**. But, similarly to the **фиг** euphemisms, the expression **блин** is completely harmless, and can be said in all but the most formal settings without risk of giving offense. It can be used anywhere **блядь** itself could be — *except* in its literal sense (i.e. you would never insult a woman by calling her a pancake!). But note that **блин** will *not* be substituted for the root **бляд-** in any of the words that follow; that is, it is not a productive euphemism in the way that **хер**, **хрен** and **фиг** are.

Блин!
BLEEN

Pancake!
(said after dropping something, for example)

Fucking... / блядь (as emphatic particle)

The emphatic particle **же** (and the much less common -**то**) lends emphasis to whatever word comes before it. It can sometimes give a sense of contrast ("meanwhile," "on the other hand," etc.). Because of this versatility, it is used *constantly* in Russian.

One way to explain the ubiquity of **блядь** in **мат** is to think of it as an emphatic particle — as an obscene stand-in for **же**. Note that in this role (due to its sheer frequency), the shortened form **бля** is often used.

Он не зн<u>а</u>ет, а <u>я</u> бля зн<u>а</u>ю! ON nye ZNA-yit, a YA blya ZNA-yoo	He doesn't know, but I fucking do! *(contrastive emphasis)*
Это т<u>ы</u> бля в<u>о</u>дку в<u>ы</u>пил. E-tuh TY blya VOT-koo VY-pil	*You're* the one who drank the fucking vodka.

It's also used emphatically after question words.

— Дав<u>а</u>й по<u>е</u>дем в Томбукт<u>у</u>. **— Куд<u>а</u> бля?** "dah-VAY pah-YE-dyim ftom-book-TOO" "koo-DA blya?"	Let's go to Timbuktu. *Where?!*

Note the alternate form of **что** — **чё** — often heard with **мат** (and not only!).

Ты чё, бля? ty CHO blya?	What are you doing? What the fuck?
Ты чё, бля, д<u>е</u>лаешь? ty CHO blya DYEH-luh-yish	What the fuck are you doing?
Ты чё, бля, вообщ<u>е</u> оху<u>е</u>л? ty CHO blya, va-ahb-SHCHYE ah-khoo-YEL	Are you fucking crazy?

Fucking... / блядь (as all-purpose filler word)

Even more generally, we can think of **блядь** — and especially the shorter form **бля** — as a filler word in a typical **мат**-laced tirade. In this usage, it has no real meaning at all; it simply "fills" pauses in speech, like the English "well" or "um" or "like." In this sense, we could also think of it as a kind of verbal punctuation mark, inserted wherever one might write a comma, semicolon, period, or exclamation point.

This usage is especially common in extended narratives (telling jokes, stories, etc.).

Here's an example of such an everyday narrative (it's obviously nothing special — the contents are quite beside the point!). English fillers like "uh" or "well" only go so far in translating this usage. A better translation might involve peppering our story with the English "fucking."

Коро́че, бля, домо́й прихожу́
бля. Смотрю́ бля в холоди́льник
бля, ви́жу: во́дку спи́здили бля.
Охуе́л бля. Зна́чит, бля...

Long story short, I fucking get home,
and I look in the fucking fridge, and
and I fucking see that my fucking
vodka's been stolen. I fucking lost my
mind. So I fucking... (etc., etc., etc.)

Sprinkling a narrative with **бля** can also convey a general sense of indignation, incredulity, hilarity, etc. — the kind of tone you'd often expect when anecdotes of this kind
are being told.

Oh for fuck's sake! / ой блядь!

Any student of Russian is familiar with the interjection "**Ой!**" — commonly used to express everything from surprise to shock to suffering. If you're in **мат** mode, you can — you guessed it! — tack on a **блядь** or **бля** for good measure.

Ой, бля, извини!   Oh, fuck, sorry about that!
oy blya, iz-vi-NEE

To act like a fucking bitch / блядничать

As a root, **блядь (бляд)** is nowhere near as productive as **ёб-** and **хуй-**; we have only two more words to consider — and even these are quite rare. But, to give one example of a verb, we have **блядничать** АЙ, meaning, quite simply, "to act like a **блядь**."

Хватит тебе блядничать!   Enough of your bitchery!
KHVAH-tit ti-BYEH BLYAD-ni-chuht'

Bitchy behavior / блядство

A noun describing bitchy behavior or debauchery generally, or a specific incident of such behavior, is the neuter noun **блядство**. This calls to mind such non-**мат** terms as **свинство** — the behavior of a **свинья** (pig) — again, either generally or in one specific instance (in the sense of a "dirty trick" or something to that effect).

Такого блядства от тебя не ожидал!   I didn't expect such bitchery from you!
tah-KO-vuh BLYAT-stvuh aht ti-BYA nye ah-zhi-DAL I didn't expect such a bitch move!

We've learned that the ubiquitous **мат** term "**хуй**" refers literally to the male reproductive organ. The female equivalent — **пизда** — is arguably more offensive, due both to its mysogynist implications and the simple fact that it's heard somewhat less often (by analogy to the English "cunt," which is arguably more offensive even than "fuck," etc. — at least in the United States; its usage in British English is somewhat different). On top of that, expressions with **хуй** often register in a vague sense, as vulgar set phrases whose literal meaning is to some extent obscured. In this sense, the phrase "**Иди в пизду**" (literally, "go into the vagina") is arguably more loaded than the standard "**Иди на хуй**." Note that the neutral term for "vagina" is **влагалище**.

Like **бдядь**, **пизда** is not nearly as productive as **хуй** and **ёб**, but several of the terms listed below are extremely common.

Cunt / пизда

This noun can, of course, refer literally to female genitalia; it can also be used to refer insultingly to a woman (just as **хуй** can refer to a man).

Старая пизда!   You stupid old cunt!
STA-ruh-yuh piz-DA!

The word can be used to denote an unpleasant situation, the middle of nowhere, etc.

Мы в пизде!   We're fucked.
my fpiz-DYEH

ПИЗДЕЦ БЛЯДЬ!

Fuck you / Иди в пизду!

As mentioned, this is a less frequently heard (and for that reason perhaps more force-ful) variant of "**Иди на хуй!**" Meaning literally "Go into the cunt," its usage is similar the English "Fuck you!" or "Go fuck yourself!"

Иди в пизду! i-DEE vpiz-DOO	Fuck you! Fuck off! *(to one person)*
Идите в пизду! i-DEE-tyeh vpiz-DOO	Fuck you! Fuck off! *(to multiple people)*

As you might have guessed, "**пошёл**" can be used here as well.

Пошёл в пизду! pah-SHOL vpiz-DOO	Fuck you! Fuck off! *(to a single male)*

A fucking disaster / пиздец

This is one of the most common expressions in **мат**, but it requires some explain-ing — it's not easy to translate! We saw a moment ago that **пизда** can mean "an unpleasant situation." The noun **пиздец** is even more emphatic — something like the English phrases "This fucking sucks!" or "This is a fucking disaster," etc. We can think of **пиздец** by analogy to **конец** (the end), as it suggests that "we're fucked, we're goners — this is the end of us!"

This is most commonly used as a one-word interjection, to express despair, disgust, frustration, etc. The variations below are heard all the time:

Пиздец! piz-DYETS	Fuck!
Пиздец какой-то! piz-DYETS ka-KOY-tuh	This fucking sucks!
Пиздец просто! piz-DYETS PRO-stuh	This is simply a fucking disaster!
Полный пиздец! POL-ny piz-DYETS	This is a total fucking disaster!

The word is often combined with the dative case, telling "who" is fucked:

Ему пиздец. yi-MOO piz-DYETS	He's fucked.
Нам пиздец. nam piz-DYETS	We're fucked.

The remaining dative pronouns are: **мне** (me), **тебе** (you sing.), **ей** (her), **вам** (you pl., or polite sing.), and **им** (them).

Пиздец may be used adverbially to suggest huge quantities, and surprise thereat:

У него пиздец сколько денег!   He's got a shit-ton of money!
oo nyi-VO piz-DYETS SKOL'-kuh DYEH-nig

Its use as an actual noun is much less common, as in this set phrase, which suggests that some great misfortune "snuck up" on someone who didn't see it coming:

Пиздец подкрался незаметно!   No one saw this shitshow coming.
piz-DYETS pahd-KRAL-syuh nyi-za-MYET-nuh

End-stressed masculine nouns

Пиздёж and **пиздец** aren't heard too often in non-nominative forms, but these are certainly possible. Note that both nouns stress all added endings!

For all practical purposes, these nouns are only used in the singular.

	sing.		sing.
nom.	пиздёж	nom.	пиздец
gen.	пиздеж**а**	gen.	пиздец**а**
acc.	пиздёж	acc.	пиздец
dat.	пиздеж**у**	dat.	пиздец**у**
prep.	пиздеж**е**	prep.	пиздец**е**
instr.	пиздеж**ом**	instr.	пиздец**ом**

Fucking bullshit / пиздёж

For whatever reason, the root **пизд-** also figures in several **мат** expressions having to do with talking bullshit. The first of these, referring to the bullshit itself (i.e. the content) or to the *activity* of bullshitting, is **пиздёж**. We can associate its form with a class of similar nouns in -**ёж**, like **платёж** (payment, paying), **грабёж** (theft, stealing), etc.

In terms of meaning, **пиздёж** can stand in for such non-**мат** expressions as **болтовня** (babbling, having "loose lips"), **сплетни** (a plural noun meaning "gossip"), **байки** (tall tales) — or the slang **брехня** (bullshit, nonsense).

Это всё пиздёж.
E-tuh fsyo piz-DYOSH

That's all a bunch of fucking bullshit.

Пиздёж and **пиздец** aren't heard too often in non-nominative forms, but these are certainly possible. Note that both are end-stressed nouns (see the box above!).

Давай без пиздежа.
dah-VAY byes piz-dyi-ZHA

Can we drop the bullshit?

A fucking bullshitter / пиздобол

A **пиздобол** is anyone who engages in **пиздёж** — someone who bullshits, or is "full of shit." Note that this is a *fixed-stress* noun — the stress never shifts!

If **пиздёж** is roughly equivalent to the non-**мат** noun **болтовня** (babbling), then **пиздобол** corresponds to **болтун** (a babbler).

Какой ты пиздобол!
kah-KOY ty piz-dah-BOL

You're so full of shit!

Все политики — пиздоболы.
fsyeh pah-LEE-ti-ki piz-dah-BO-ly

All politicians are full of shit.

To talk bullshit / пизд<u>е</u>ть

Finally, we have the verb that goes with **пизд<u>ё</u>ж** and **пиздоб<u>о</u>л**: **пизд<u>е</u>ть**, an imperfective verb meaning "to talk bullshit."

In our system of verb types, **пизд<u>е</u>ть** is classified as a "**E**" noun (read: "yeh") because of its stem vowel. But note how the stem vowel is lost in the present tense, where **E** verbs work exactly like **И** verbs: they take the "**и**" endings, and mutate in the **я** form only, whenever a mutation is possible.

пизд<u>е</u>ть Eᵉⁿᵈ: to talk bullshit (imperf.)	
пизж<u>у</u>	I'm talking bullshit
пизд<u>ишь</u>	you're talking bullshit
пизд<u>ит</u>	he, she is talking bullshit
пизд<u>им</u>	we're talking bullshit
пизд<u>ите</u>	you're talking bullshit
пизд<u>ят</u>	they're talking bullshit
пизд<u>и</u>!	talk bullshit!
пизд<u>е</u>л	he was talking bullshit
пизд<u>е</u>ла	she was talking bullshit
пизд<u>е</u>ли	they were talking bullshit

The letter "**д**" can mutate in Russian, to a "**ж**" — and so it does here, in the **я** form only.

Note, meanwhile, that the *past*-tense forms *do* retain the stem vowel "**e**." Here, as with the vast majority of Russian verbs, the past tense is derived directly from the infinitive, by replacing the infinitive ending -**ть** with the past-tense marker -**л**.

The verb **пизд<u>е</u>ть** corresponds to non-**мат** verbs like **болт<u>а</u>ть** АЙ (to babble) or **врать** (to lie, tell tall tales, etc).

Что ты пизд<u>и</u>шь?! shto ty piz-DEESH	Why are you talking this bullshit?
Не пизд<u>и</u>! nye piz-DEE	Don't talk bullshit!
Хв<u>а</u>тит теб<u>е</u> пизд<u>е</u>ть! KHVAH-tit ti-BYEH piz-DYET'	That's enough bullshit from you!
Я не пизж<u>у</u>! ya nye piz-ZHOO (note: the **з** is often not pronounced in this combination)	I'm not talking bullshit!
Теб<u>е</u> пизд<u>я</u>т. ti-BYEH piz-DYAT	People are bullshitting you. ("they are bullshitting to you")

To fucking steal / сп<u>и</u>здить

Meaning "to steal," the aspectual pair **п<u>и</u>здить** И / **сп<u>и</u>здить** И is the **мат** equivalent of **красть** Дᵉⁿᵈ (крад<u>у</u>, крад<u>ё</u>шь, etc.) / **укр<u>а</u>сть** Д: to steal. This is another good example of a **мат** term that can't be interpreted literally; we simply learn the meaning, and note that it's built from the vulgar **пизд-**. Its prefix **с-** calls to mind the verb **стащ<u>и</u>ть** И: to swipe, pilfer, "drag away."

Take a moment to distinguish between the **Е** verb **пиздеть** and the **И** verb **пиздить**. First, the former is end-stressed, while the second is stem-stressed. Second, these verbs are wonderful examples of how **Е** and **И** verbs work exactly the same in their present-tense forms: both take the "**и**" endings, and both mutate in the **я** form only whenever a mutation is possible. Thus, the only thing distinguishing the present-tense forms of **пиздеть** and **пиздить** is the placement of the stress!

Here are all forms for the aspectual pair **пиздить** И / **спиздить** И:

пиздить И: to steal (imperfective)		**спиздить** И: to steal (perfective)	
пи<u>з</u>ж**у**	I'm fucking stealing	спи<u>з</u>ж**у**	I'll fucking steal
пи<u>з</u>д**ишь**	you're fucking stealing	спи<u>з</u>д**ишь**	you'll fucking steal
пи<u>з</u>д**ит**	he, she is fucking stealing	спи<u>з</u>д**ит**	he, she'll fucking steal
пи<u>з</u>д**им**	we're fucking stealing	спи<u>з</u>д**им**	we'll fucking steal
пи<u>з</u>д**ите**	you're fucking stealing	спи<u>з</u>д**ите**	you'll fucking steal
пи<u>з</u>д**ят**	they're fucking stealing	спи<u>з</u>д**ят**	they'll fucking steal
пи<u>з</u>ди!	fucking steal!	спи<u>з</u>ди!	fucking steal!
пи<u>з</u>дил	he was fucking stealing	спи<u>з</u>дил	he fucking stole
пи<u>з</u>дила	she was fucking stealing	спи<u>з</u>дила	she fucking stole
пи<u>з</u>дили	they were fucking stealing	спи<u>з</u>дили	they fucking stole

The usage is pretty obvious! For example:

Кто спи<u>з</u>дил мо<u>и</u> час<u>ы</u>?
kto SPEEZ-dil mah-EE chah-SY

Who stole my fucking watch?

To beat the shit out of / отп<u>и</u>здить

The verb **пиздить** И has another meaning: to beat the shit out of someone. In this meaning, the perfective has a different prefix: **от-**, giving the aspectual pair **пиздить** И / **отпиздить** И.

The basic non-**мат** equivalent is **бить** Ь (бью, бьёшь) / **изб<u>и</u>ть** Ь (изобь<u>ю</u>, изобь<u>ё</u>шь): to beat / to beat up.

Ег<u>о</u> отп<u>и</u>здили.
yi-VO aht-PEEZ-di-li

Someone beat the shit out of him.

Let's give an example using a "hypothetical" (more commonly known as a "conditional") construction. Thankfully, these forms are quite simple in Russian: just combine the "hypothetical particle" **бы** with the past-tense form of the verb (note that hypothetical constructions actually *lack tense*, but in any case they look like past-tense forms):

Он бы теб<u>я</u> отп<u>и</u>здил.
on by ti-BYAH aht-PEEZ-dil

He'd beat the shit out of you.

To beat the shit out of / дать пизды

There's another way to say: "to beat the shit out of someone." Literally, "to give some pussy to someone" (this would be used with the dative case).

Дава̲й дади̲м ему̲ пизды̲.   Let's beat the shit out of him.
da-VAY dah-DEEM yi-MOO piz-DY

To beat the shit out of / дать пиздюле̲й

But wait, there's more! A synonym for **дать пизды** is **дать пиздюле̲й** — a set expression also involving a partitive genitive (plural) of **пиздю̲ль**, я̲. This word, meaning a beating or other unpleasant predicament, is rarely used in the singular.

Дава̲й дади̲м ему̲ пиздюле̲й.   Let's beat the shit out of him.
da-VAY dah-DEEM yi-MOO piz-dyoo-LYEY

Conjugating "to give" (and АВАЙ verbs)

The two phrases above involve the verb "to give," whose pair is **дава̲ть** АВАЙ / **дать**. This is surely one of the most common verbs in Russian — and most frequently mis-conjugated! The imperfective **дава̲ть** is an "**АВАЙ**" verb under our system; in the present tense, their stem contracts, giving, for example **я даю̲** (*not* я дава̲ю!); meanwhile, they behave normally in the past tense.

The perfective verb **дать** is quite simply *irregular*, and must be learned. Note that its conjugated forms (like all such perfective forms) have *future* meaning.

The only remaining АВАЙ verbs in the entire language are all *prefixed* forms of **дава̲ть** (like передава̲ть: to hand over), -**знава̲ть** (like узнава̲ть: to find out; recognize), and -**става̲ть** (like встава̲ть: to get up, rise). Note that the latter two only occur with prefixes.

дава̲ть АВАЙ: to give (imperfective)		**дать**: to give (perfective)	
даю̲	I'm giving	дам	I'll give
даёшь	you're giving	дашь	you'll give
даёт	he, she is giving	даст	he, she'll give
даём	we're giving	дади̲м	we'll give
даёте	you're giving	дади̲те	you'll give
даю̲т	they're giving	даду̲т	they'll give
дава̲й!	give!	дай!	give!
дава̲л	he was giving	дал	he gave
дава̲ла	she was giving	дала̲	she gave
дава̲ли	they were giving	да̲ли	they gave

One may hear the plural **пиздюли** used with other verbs:

Х<u>о</u>чешь пиздюл<u>е</u>й? Wanna fucking knuckle sandwich?
KHO-chish piz-dyoo-LYEY

To get the fuck out of here / пиздов<u>а</u>ть

The pair **пиздов<u>а</u>ть** ОВА / **попиздов<u>а</u>ть** ОВА means "to go" or, in the perfective, to "get going," to "head off." Like so many **мат** expressions, it may be used crudely or emphatically (i.e. "get the fuck out of here," "get your ass moving," etc.), or quite neutrally, as a **мат** stand-in for "to go" or "to run."

See the box below for a note on conjugation.

Бля, пор<u>а</u> пиздов<u>а</u>ть на раб<u>о</u>ту. Fuck, it's time to go to work.
blya, pah-RAH piz-dah-VAT' na rah-BO-too

A fucking slacker / распизд<u>я</u>й

The noun **распизд<u>я</u>й** refers to a lazy, unreliable, apathetic person. The feminine version would be **распизд<u>я</u>йка**. A good non-**мат** equivalent is **разгильд<u>я</u>й**. The state or activity of being this person is **распид<u>я</u>йство** (**разгильд<u>я</u>йство**).

Наш н<u>о</u>вый сотр<u>у</u>дник — распизд<u>я</u>й. Our new co-worker is a fucking slacker.
nash NO-vy sah-TROOD-nik ras-piz-DYAY

Conjugating OBA verbs

In these extremely common verbs, the stem suffix **ОВА** collapses to "y" in conjugated forms (similarly to how **АВАЙ** verbs collapse — see to the left!)

пиздов<u>а</u>ть ОВА: to go (imperf.)		попиздов<u>а</u>ть ОВА: to go (perf.)	
пизд<u>у</u>ю	I'm going	попизд<u>у</u>ю	I'll go
пизд<u>у</u>ешь	you're going	попизд<u>у</u>ешь	you'll go
пизд<u>у</u>ет	he, she is going	попизд<u>у</u>ет	he, she'll go
пизд<u>у</u>ем	we're going	попизд<u>у</u>ем	we'll go
пизд<u>у</u>ете	you're going	попизд<u>у</u>ете	you'll go
пизд<u>у</u>ют	they're going	попизд<u>у</u>ют	they'll go
пизд<u>у</u>й!	go!	попизд<u>у</u>й!	go!
пиздов<u>а</u>л	he was going	попиздов<u>а</u>л	he went
пиздов<u>а</u>ла	she was going	попиздов<u>а</u>ла	she went
пиздов<u>а</u>ли	they were going	попиздов<u>а</u>ли	they went

Fucking great / пизд<u>а</u>тый

Finally, we have an adjective: **пизд<u>а</u>тый**, meaning "fucking great." Like the the adjectives we saw earlier (**ху<u>ё</u>вый**, **оху<u>е</u>нный**, **оху<u>и</u>тельный**), it can be used in a short (adverbial) form as well:

— **Как ты себ<u>я</u> ч<u>у</u>вствуешь?**	"How do you feel?"
— **Пизд<u>а</u>то!**	"Fucking great."
— kak ty si-BYAH CHOOST-voo-yish	
— piz-DAH-tuh	

Our final **мат** root is almost never heard in its basic noun form — **мудо**, meaning "testicle." The actual plural of this word — **муде** — is a peculiar one, derived from archaic "dual" forms. Once upon a time, Slavic languages had three grammatical numbers: singular, plural, and *dual* — the latter being used for "two" of anything, including body parts that come in plairs; both nouns and pronouns, and the verbs that went with them, had special "dual" endings! This "strange" form may be discarded in favor of more conventional-looking plurals, like **муда**. In any case, the plural of this word (testicles) might be translated as "scrotum" or "ballsack."

Again, the term **муда** itself is rarely heard. To refer literally to the scrotum, the singular noun **мошонка** (an official anatomical term) may be used — or, much more commonly, the slang **яйца**, whose literal meaning is "eggs" (it's the plural of **яйцо**), and whose usage resembles that of the English "balls" or "nuts."

Because **муда** itself is rarely used, this chapter will stick to terms derived from **муд-** — and though there are only a few of them, they're extremely common. In much the same way that **пизд-** is associated with babbling, stealing and "bitchy" behavior, the root **муд-** has one dominant meaning: total stupidity.

Fucking idiot / мудак

This is one of the most common insults in **мат**, equivalent to non-**мат** terms like **дурак** or **придурок** (idiot). Its usage is pretty self-explanatory!

Like **пиздёж** and **пиздец** (discussed earlier), **мудак** is an *end*-stressed masculine noun. Note how all the endings in the table to the right are stressed. This is a great word to practice this stress pattern, since it is used often in just about every case!

	sing.	pl.
nom.	мудак	мудаки
gen.	мудака	мудаков
acc.	мудака	мудаков
dat.	мудаку	мудакам
prep.	мудаке	мудаках
instr.	мудаком	мудаками

Here are just a few simple examples, in various cases:

Какой ты мудак! kah-KOY ty moo-DAK	You're such a fucking idiot!
Твои друзья мудаки. tvah-EE drooz-YA moo-dah-KEE	Your friends are fucking idiots.
Не хочу работать с мудаками. nye kha-CHOO rah-BO-tuht' s moo-dah-KA-mee	I don't want to work with fucking idiots.
Он назвал меня мудаком. on nah-ZVAL mi-NYAH moo-dah-KOM	He called me a fucking idiot.

Fucking idiot / мудило

This is a less-common synonym of **мудак** — an idiotic or otherwise unpleasant person. I can't resist sharing a little New Year's poem I once heard; it exists in many variants, but they all go something like this, culminating in our newest word:

— Здравствуй, Дедушка Мороз, Борода из ваты! Ты подарки нам принёс, Педераст горбатый?	"Greetings, Grandfather Frost, Beard of cotton! Did you bring us presents, You hunchbacked pederast?"
— Нет, подарков не принёс, Денег не хватило!	"No, I didn't bring any presents, There wasn't enough money."
— Так зачем же ты пришёл, Ватное мудило?	"Then what did you come here for, You cotton motherfucker?"

Here's a transliteration:

ZDRAST-vooy, DYEH-doosh-kuh ma-ROZ, / buh-rah-DA iz VA-ty! / Ty pa-DAR-ki nam pri-NYOS, / Pi-di-RAST gar-BA-ty? / nyet, pa-DAR-kuhf nye pri-NYOS / DYEH-nig nye kva-TEE-luh! / tak za-CHEM zhe ty pri-SHOL, / VAT-nuh-yeh moo-DEE-luh?

МУДАКИ ВЫ ВСЕ!

Ёбанное муди́ло!   Fucking idiot!
YO-buh-nuh-yeh moo-DEE-luh

Fucking idiotism / муди́зм

The **-изм** suffix creates an "-ism" noun, describing the state or activity of being and acting like a **муда́к** or **муди́ло**.

By the way, this is a *stem*-stressed noun — see the box below!

По́лный муди́зм бля!   This is total fucking idiotism!
POL-ny moo-DEE-zuhm blya

Stem-stressed nouns

Many Russian nouns have tricky stress patterns, like the end-stressed nouns we've already looked at. But it's reassuring to remember that the vast majority of Russian nouns *never shift* their stress — it is "fixed" somewhere on the stem, and never moves around when we add various case endings.

	sing.
nom.	муди́зм
gen.	муди́зм**а**
acc.	муди́зм
dat.	муди́зм**у**
prep.	муди́зм**е**
instr.	муди́зм**ом**

Here are few extremely handy guidelines for spotting nouns that are stem-stressed. They include:

1. Almost all **borrowed nouns**, including those with borrowed suffiixes like **-изм** (коммуни́зм) or **-ист** (коммуни́ст). Of course, these include муди́зm.

2. All **feminine nouns** (native or borrowed, doesn't matter!) whose nominative singular is stem-stressed — that is, not stressed on the ending **-а** or **-я**. For example: **кни́га** (book), **ко́шка** (cat), **кварти́ра** (apartment) — the list goes on and on.

3. All so-called **special soft** nouns, including (rare) masculines in **-ий** like **ге́ний** (genius), and extremely common feminines in **-ия** like **револю́ция** (revolution) and neuters in **-ие** like **мне́ние** (opinion).

4. The fourth group, while a bit harder to spot until an intermediate to advanced stage of study, includes most masculine nouns built **with prefixes** — many of which correspond to a prefixed verb. For example: **вопро́с** (question), **отве́т** (answer), **прие́зд** (arrival), **вы́ход** (exit), etc. There are exceptions, such as **по́езд** (train), which has end-stress in the plural (followings its nom. pl. **поезда́**).

Noun stress is an extremely complex topic in Russian, but the tips here will allow you to decline a great number of nouns with confidence.

Fucking idiotic / мудацкий

Now for the adjectival form of these words: **мудацкий** describes anything proper to or characteristic of a **мудак** or **мудизм**.

Выключи эту мудацкую песню!   Turn off that fucking idiotic song!
VY-klyoo-chi E-too moo-DATS-koo-yoo PYES-nyoo

Ты ведёшь мудацкий образ жизни.   You lifestyle is fucking idiotic.
ty vi-DYOSH moo-DATS-ky O-bruhs ZHEEZ-ni

The **и т. д.** in the heading stands for "**и так далее**" — "and so forth," "etc." We've come now to a perhaps controversial point in our discussion of мат — namely, where exactly does **мат** end? Generally, we can certainly say that there is a range of "bad words" in Russian that one wouldn't use in polite company or formal situations. Some are almost certainly as crude and as offensive as the **мат** vocabulary we've studied thus far. Yet, such words are not necessarily classified as **мат** in the strictest sense.

It's essential to note that there is no consensus here; if you ask a number of Russians which words constitute **мат**, you're likely to get varying answers. Here as elsewhere in one's langauge study, it's a good idea to get a range of opinions; the view of any particular native speaker may be biased, or at the very least incomplete.

Speaking of opinions: as far as this book is concerned, we've reached the end of **мат**. When I was first introduced to **мат** by Russian friends, they restricted it to the five roots surveyed thus far: **хуй, ёб, блядь, пизд-**, and **муд-** (the latter with slight hesitation). After years of subsequent study, I would support this view. Why?

To me, the defining criterion is that of word formation — the "productivity" of **мат** roots. As we've seen, the real expressivity of **мат** lies in the way many words with widely disparate meanings can be created from a single obscene root; the resulting vocabulary can be applied to almost anything. This is what makes **мат** a kind of language unto itself — one that is "richer" than English obscenity.

Surely no Russian speaker would dispute that the first four roots (**хуй**, **ёб**, **блядь**, **пизд**-) all constitute **мат**. Consider the following line from Leningrad's song **День рождения** (Birthday), a cosmic *cri de coeur* that unites all four elements of **мат**:

А я вот день рожде̲нья	Well, I refuse to celebrate
Не бу̲ду справля̲ть.	My birthday.
Всё заеба̲ло!	I'm fucking sick of everything!
Пиздец на̲ хуй блядь!	Fuck it all to hell!

Transliteration: A ya vot dyen' razh-DYEN'-yuh / nye BOO-doo sprav-LYAT' / vsyoh za-yi-BA-luh / piz-DYETS NA khooy blyat'!

Meanwhile, the root **муд**- is worth special consideration. I suspect many would not classify it as **мат**. I would, according to the criterion of word formation, even though it is not nearly as productive as some **мат** roots. Admittedly, this relative lack of productivity — and the fact that such derived terms as **мудак** are arguably not as offensive as other **мат** vocabulary — do leave this open to debate. Of course, the fact that it does refer literally to genitalia is another argument for classifying it as **мат**.

Meanwhile, let's consider a word like **сука** (female dog; bitch). I have no doubt that some Russians would classify this as **мат**, by virtue of the simple fact that it's a "very bad word," and a highly charged (misogynist) insult. Furthermore, it's the kind of word one hears all the time in **мат** tirades, including as kind of simple interjection or filler word with little or no real meaning beyond "cursing." I would certainly agree, but I (following my friends) would not classify it as **мат** because it is not productive. Yes, it yields the term **сукин сын** (son of a bitch), but this is just a standard possessive-adjective construction, not an entirely new word built off the root.

Simply put: in Russian, as in any language, the question of which words are "curse words" is to some degree subjective.

With all this in mind, let's complete our studies with a list of basic "bad words" that we haven't classified as **мат** proper. The reasons for including this "epilogue" are several: 1) any Russian learner should know these words, and know that they are indeed "bad words"; 2) to varying degrees, these words are very likely to be heard when people are speaking **мат**, regardless of whether or not we classify the words themselves as **мат**; 3) English speakers should understand that some words we might assume to be **мат** (based on English) are ultimately quite harmless — one example being **говно̲** (shit), which, though it is certainly not to be used at the dinner table, is definitely not **мат**. The same is true, in my opinion, for all the words in this chapter.

Finally, just because a naughty word may not be considered **мат** doesn't mean that it can't be "productive." Obviously, most Russian roots produce a number of different words, and many of the following words are no exception; for example, **говно** gives **говённый** and **говнюк**. At the same time, their productivity is far more limited both in terms of number and in range of meanings than such undisputed **мат** roots as **хуй** and **ёб**. This fact is even reflected in the ease of translating **говно** (shit) terms into English: **говённый** (shitty), **говнюк** (shithead).

Bitch / су́ка

As noted earlier, this is the exact equivalent of the English "bitch" — a term for a female dog that can be applied insultingly to women (or, in fact, to anyone as a term of contempt). It can certainly be used literally in both of these meanings. Again, it often features in outbursts of **мат**, even though its own status as **мат** may be debatable. Like so many **мат** expressions, it too may be used as a simple interjection or filler word, in which case its literal meaning is of little import (see the second example).

Почему́ она́ така́я су́ка?! pah-chi-MOO ah-NAH ta-KA-yuh SOO-kuh	Why is she such a bitch!
Ёб твою́ мать су́ка блядь! YOB tva-YOO mat' SOO-kuh blyat'	Fucketty-fuck-fuck-fuck...

Son of a bitch / су́кин сын

I've heard Russian learners translate the English "son of a bitch" using the genitive, and arriving at "**сын су́ки**." Unfortunately, this is not the Russian idiom! Instead of the genitive, a special feminine "possessive adjective" form is used. These use the suffix -**ин**, and follow a somewhat unusual declension similar to last names ending in -**ин** (see below). Compare another example: **ма́менькин сыно́к** (momma's boy, formed

Possessive adjectives from nouns with feminine endings

These can be formed from "familiar" names, which take feminine endings (like **Бо́ря** or **Ма́ша**) — and from ordinary feminine nouns, like **ба́бушка** (e.g. **ба́бушкин дом**: grandma's house). These decline like long adjectives, *except* in the forms marked by the black boxes, which show noun endings.

	masculine	feminine	neuter	plural
nom.	су́кин	су́кина	су́кино	су́кины
gen.	су́кина (-ого)	су́киной	су́кина (-ого)	су́киных
acc.	су́кин	су́кину	су́кино	су́кины
anim.	су́кина (-ого)			су́киных
dat.	су́кину	су́киной	су́кину	су́киным
prep.	су́кином	су́киной	су́кином	су́киных
instr.	су́кин**ым**	су́киной	су́кин**ым**	су́кин**ыми**

from **маменька**). These possessive adjectives can be formed from any feminine noun, including names — even "familiar" forms of male names taking feminine endings, such as **Миша** (from **Михаил**). For example: **Мишин отец** (Misha's dad), **Мишина машина** (Misha's car), or **Мишины джинсы** (Misha's jeans).

In case you're wondering, "daughter of a bitch" would be **сукина дочь**.

Убью этого сукина сына.	I'll kill the son of a bitch.
oo-BYOO E-tuh-vuh SOO-ki-nuh SY-nuh	

Because of how unusual this declension pattern is, one may also hear a long-form adjectival ending in this example: "**сукиного сына.**"

Shit / говно

Few Russian speakers (if any at all) would classify this word as **мат**; its meaning has nothing to do with fucking or genitalia, and, although crude, it's not considered nearly as bad as real **мат**. Even the English "shit" may possibly sound worse. Note that there is a milder term, **дерьмо**, which corresponds roughly to the English "crap."

It's very important to note that while the English "shit" is a common interjection ("Oh, SHIT!"), the Russian **говно** is not used in this way. That is, if a Russian utters the one-word sentence, "**Говно!**" then it would presumably mean something like "That's a bunch of shit," or "That's bullshit."

We might note that a more neutral term for excrement is the plural-only noun **фекалии** (feces), or **кал** (something like Enligh "dung"). Both are rarely heard.

Что за говно!	What is this shit?
shto za gav-NO	

Of course, **говно** is a neuter noun that is fully declinable:

Мы тонем в говне.	We're drowning in shit.
my TO-nyim v gav-NYEH	*(prepositional case)*

Не тронь говно, не воняет.	Don't touch shit, and it won't smell!
nye tron' gav-NO, nye vahn-YA-yit	*(accusative case)*

The second example is a **пословица** (proverb); there are multiple versions of it. It means something like "Let a sleeping dog lie," i.e. leave something alone and it won't become a problem. I am perennially amazed at how few students seem to understand the proverb's meaning — have they never stepped in dog shit?! Let me explain:

Without question, a fresh pile of shit smells bad. But as it sits around, drying out, crusting over, etc. it become less noxious — unless, of course, you stir it up, disturbing and exposing its putrid core. Hence, the meaning of the proverb.

Shitty / говённый

The meaning here is clear. Like the noun it derives from, it's not a very bad — roughly on par with such euphemistic **мат** terms as **хреновый**.

Это самый говённый ресторан в городе. That's the shittiest restaurant in town.
E-tuh SA-my gah-VYO-ny res-tah-RAN VGO-ruh-dyeh

Shithead / говнюк

This end-stressed noun is comparable to the English "shithead." The feminine equivalent is **говнючка**. Since these nouns refer to people, they are *animate* (see below).

Пошли этого говнюка куда подальше. Send that shithead "somewhere further."
pa-SHLEE E-tuh-vuh gav-nyoo-KA koo-DA pah-DAL'-she   (that is, tell him to go **на хуй**)

Animacy and the accusative case

Now that we've seen a variety of animate nouns, let's review a very confusing topic: the *accusative* case.

In short, there is only one *distinctly accusative* ending: that of **feminine singular** nouns. Remember a simple rule: -**a** becomes -**y**, and -**я** becomes -**ю**. Thus: книга → **книгу**, подруга → **подругу**, неделя → **неделю**.

Aside from these feminine singular forms, *all remaining accusative* forms look like either the **nominative** or the **genitive**.

The accusatives of all **inanimate** nouns (masculine or neuter) look like the **nominative**. Thus: окно → **окно**, стол → **стол**. Same goes for plurals!

The accusatives of **animate** nouns look like the **genitive**. Thus, to take a masculine example: студент → **студента**, and plural студенты → **студентов**.

Now, back to **feminine animates**: they too look like genitives in the plural, but follow the general rule in the singular. Hence: сука → **суку** and суки → **сук**.

	sing.	sing.	pl.	sing.	pl.
nom.	говно	говнюк	говнюки	сука	суки
gen.	говна	говнюка	говнюков	суки	сук
acc.	говно	говнюка	говнюков	суку	сук
dat.	говну	говнюку	говнюкам	суке	сукам
prep.	говне	говнюке	говнюках	суке	суках
instr.	говном	говнюком	говнюками	сукой	суками

To shit / срать

The verb **срать** means, quite simply, "to shit." It follows the somewhat unusual "n/sA" conjugation pattern (see below). It has two perfectives with slightly different meanings, giving us the following two aspectual pairs:

срать n/sA / **посрать** n/sA	**срать** n/sA / **насрать** n/sA на что
to shit / to take a shit	to shit on

The first variant (**посрать**) describes the act of shitting generally, or taking a shit:

Мне посрать надо.   I need to take a shit.
mnyeh pah-SRAT' NA-duh

The second (whose perfective is **насрать**) means literally "to shit onto," and is followed by **на** + the accusative case.

Кот всё время срёт на ковёр.   The cat is always shitting on the carpet.
kot fsyo VRYE-myuh sryot na kah-VYOR

Aside from this literal meaning, the phrase is often used to convey indifference or contempt. In this sense, it recalls the common expression "to spit on" (**плевать** ОВА / **наплевать** ОВА (or **плюнуть** НУ) на что).

Мне на это насрать.   I don't give a shit about that.
mnye na E-tuh na-SRAT'   (literally: I could shit on that)

Conjugating "to shit" and "to piss"

While **ссать** is irregular, **срать** follows the "**n/sA**" (say "en es ah") pattern. These verbs are built from a non-syllabic root consisting of two consonants (represented in the tag by the dummy consonants "n" and "s," with a "/" instead of a vowel), followed by the stem vowel "a." Compare: **ждать** n/sA: to wait.

срать n/sA: to shit (imperfective)		**ссать**: to piss (imperfective)	
сру	I'm shitting	ссу	I'm pissing
срёшь	you're shitting	ссышь	you're pissing
срёт	he, she is shitting	ссыт	he, she is pissing
срём	we're shitting	ссым	we're pissing
срёте	you're shitting	ссыте	you're pissing
срут	they're shitting	ссут	they're pissing
сри!	shit!	ссы!	piss!
срал	he was shitting	ссал	he was pissing
срала	she was shitting	ссала	she was pissing
срали	they were shitting	ссали	they were pissing

The Russian for "to defecate" is **испражня́ться** АЙ / **испражни́ться** И^{end}; hence the noun **испражне́ние** (defecation, excrement). The euphemism on par with the English "to go number two" is **ходи́ть** И / **сходи́ть** И **по большо́й нужде́**: to "make a round trip (to the bathroom) on account of the large need (**нужда́**)."

To fucking lose, to shit oneself / просра́ть, обосра́ться

We should list two reasonably common prefixed forms derived from **срать**:

просира́ть АЙ / посра́ть n/sA	обсира́ться АЙ / обосра́ться n/sA
to "shit through," lose, waste	to "shit oneself," be a coward

Literally meaning to "shit through," the first pair means to lose or waste in a disgraceful manner. In the sense of "wasting," it happens to recall the English "to piss away" (one's money, etc.). For example:

Ты опя́ть все де́ньги просра́л? ty ah-PYAT' fsyeh DYEN'-gi prah-SRAL	Did you piss away all your money again?
На́ша кома́нда просра́ла. NA-shuh ka-MAHN-duh prah-SRA-luh	Our team fucking lost.

The second pair, meaning literally to "shit oneself" is commonly used to describe being a coward — "shitting one's pants" with fear, etc.

Я чуть не обосра́лся! ya choot' nye uh-bah-SRAL-sya	I almost shat my pants!

To piss / ссать

The verb **ссать** has an irregular conjugation (see the box to the left). This verb too involves two aspectual pairs — one for simple "taking a piss," one for "pissing on."

ссать / посса́ть	ссать / насса́ть
to piss / to take a piss	to piss on

As with **срать**, we can also create a prefixed verb meaning **обоссыва́ться** АЙ / **обосса́ться**, meaning "to piss one's pants."

Мне на́до посса́ть. mnye NA-duh pah-SSAT'	I need to take a piss.

The term for "to urinate" is **мочи́ться** И^{shift} / **помочи́ться** И; "urine" is **моча́**. The euphemism for "going number one" is **ходи́ть** И / **сходи́ть** И **по ма́лой нужде́**: to "make a round trip (to the bathroom) on account of the small need (**нужда́**)."

There are other ways to talk about pissing. Cognate with English "to piss" is the verb **писать** (note the box below regarding conjugation!); the pair is **писать** АЙ / **пописать** АЙ. Note also the term **писсуар** (borrowed from French), meaning "urinal." Also common is the perfective verb **отлить** Ь: to take a piss (from **лить** Ь: to pour).

Are you writing or pissing?

These two verbs are easily confused... and show how important it is to distinguish between conjugation types (without being tricked by infinitives). Note also that the only thing distinguishing these infinitives is the stress!

писать A^shift: to write (imperfective)		**писать** АЙ: to piss (imperfective)	
пиш**у**	I'm writing	писа**ю**	I'm pissing
пиш**ешь**	you're writing	писа**ешь**	you're pissing
пиш**ет**	he, she is writing	писа**ет**	he, she is pissing
пиш**ем**	we're writing	писа**ем**	we're pissing
пиш**ете**	you're writing	писа**ете**	you're pissing
пиш**ут**	they're writing	писа**ют**	they're pissing
пиш**и**!	write!	писа**й**!	piss!
писал	he was writing	писал	he was pissing
писала	she was writing	писала	she was pissing
писали	they were writing	писали	they were pissing

Ass(hole) / жопа

This is yet another word that's unquestionably crude, yet probably not considered **мат**... despite the fact that several of the expressions below ("Go into the asshole!") closely resemble **мат** expressions.

This noun can refer literally to the asshole, or, more loosely, to the ass (compare the non-**мат** nouns **зад** or **задница**, which refer quite literally to one's "rear").

| **Он на жопу упал.** | He fell no his ass. |
| on na ZHO-poo oo-PAL | |

| **Бля, жопа болит!** | My ass hurts! |
| blya, ZHO-puh bah-LEET | |

More figuratively, it can also denote an unpleasant situation (much like **пизда**):

| **Мы в глубокой жопе.** | We're in a deep asshole. |
| my vgloo-BO-kuhy ZHO-pyeh | |

Just as we can send people "onto a dick" and "into a pussy," we can send them "into an asshole."

Иди в ж<u>о</u>пу! i-DEE VZHO-poo	Fuck you! Fuck off!

Пошёл в ж<u>о</u>пу! pah-SHOL VZHO-poo	Fuck you! Fuck off! *(said to a single male)*

Note the phrase **в ж<u>о</u>пу пь<u>я</u>ный** — "drunk into the asshole" (that is, fucking wasted).

Он оп<u>я</u>ть в ж<u>о</u>пу пьян. on ah-PYAT' VZHO-poo p'yan.	He's shit-faced drunk again.

There are a few reasonably common words derived from жопа as a root. Take, for example, the adjectives **хитрож<u>о</u>пый** (clever, smart-assed), **головож<u>о</u>пый** (idiotic, ass-headed), or **толстож<u>о</u>пый** (fat-assed).

Pederast / педер<u>а</u>ст

Earlier (in our Christmas jingle) we saw Grandfather Frost (i.e. Santa Claus) accused of pederasty. Or did we? In Russian, the term **педер<u>а</u>ст** has come to be a pejorative term for gay men — and though I'd prefer to banish the term from this book, it is so commonly used with **мат** that it simply can't go unmentioned. Again, to be clear: while this is a very insulting term, it is not **мат** properly speaking. At the same time, the fact that this is arguably the go-to insult (directed at men) suggests a widespread homophobia within the more general taboo on sex and genitalia that colors **мат** in general.

Note first of all that while **педер<u>а</u>ст** itself may certainly be heard, its more common variants are **пидарас** and, especially, **пид<u>о</u>р**. Secondly: while there is no denying that these nouns may all be used as explicitly homophobic insults, they are used so often *as* insults that their original meaning may (arguably) have become obscured. In this sense, the closest English equivalent might be "motherfucker" — while its literal meaning is obvious, it's not clear that speakers think literally of "one who fucks his mother" every time they utter this word.

Here is an example of a typical outburst to show what we mean; it makes little sense to translate every word literally. In essence, this is just one I'M GONNA FUCK YOU UP.

Я теб<u>я</u> в<u>ы</u>ебу, н<u>а</u> хуй блядь, пид<u>о</u>р блядь, ёб тво<u>ю</u> мать, с<u>у</u>ка блядь!
ya ti-BYA VY-yi-boo NA khooy blyat', PEE-duhr blyat', YOP tva-yoo mat' SOO-kuh blyat'

To fuck / тр<u>а</u>хать

What about basic verbs for "having sex," aside from the **мат** verb **еб<u>а</u>ть / в<u>ы</u>ебать**?

There are the harmless **занима́ться се́ксом** АЙ / **заня́ться се́ксом** Й/Мᵉⁿᵈ (займу́сь, займёшься), meaning "to have sex" (literally, to "occupy oneself with sex"); or **спать** (сплю, спишь) / **переспа́ть**: to sleep (with...). Both can be followed by **с** ("with") + the instrumental case.

Then, there's the crude — but non-**мат** — verb **тра́хать**; it's comparable to the English "to bang," and can be followed by a direct object. Add the reflexive particle, and we get reciprocity, as in "they're banging each other." Here are these two pairs:

тра́хать АЙ / **тра́хнуть** НУ кого	**тра́хаться** АЙ / **тра́хнуться** НУ
to bang	to bang each other

Another fairly common non-**мат** verb for "to fuck" (both literally and, more often, in the figurative sense of "to fuck someone up") is **поиме́ть** ЕЙ — literally, to "possess" or "take." This is a milder but still highly insulting substitute for **вы́ебать**.

Мы вас всех поиме́ем.	We're gonna fuck you (all) up.
my vas fsyekh puh-i-MYEH-yim	

Things to call people...

What about some common insults, for both men and women? Here are just a few; note again that, while certainly offensive, these are not **мат**!

men	women
сво́лочь, и (fem.!): scum	**сте́рва**: bitch
подо́н(о)к: asshole	**шлю́ха**: whore
ублю́д(о)к: bastard	**ку́рва**: whore

"Animal" vocabulary

Another sub-set of offensive language that may often be used in conjunction with **мат** might be called "animal" vocabulary. Of course, certain animal names can be used as insults (which may seem harmless — but I once saw a guy get beaten up and left on the side of the road by a bus driver after calling him a "goat"). But describing a person's face like that of an animal, or using verbs that normally describe the way an animal eats or dies can also be insulting. Here are a few common examples:

коз(ё)л: goat (said of a man)   **ры́ло**: (pig's) snout, ugly face
свинья́: pig   **ро́жа**: ugly face
коро́ва: cow (said of a woman)

Now for a couple of verbs:

жрать n/sA / **сожрать** n/sA: to eat   (compare есть / съесть)

дохнуть (НУ) / **сдохнуть** (НУ): to die   (compare умир_а_ть АЙ / умер_е_ть /Р)

Since these verbs both have tricky conjugations, the patters are given below. Note that the type **(НУ)** refers to "disappearing НУ verbs," in which the suffix НУ drops out in past-tense forms.

жрать n/sA: to eat (imperfective)		**дохнуть** (НУ): to die (imperfective)	
жр**у**	I'm eating	дохн**у**	I'm dying
жр**ёшь**	you're eating	дохн**ешь**	you're dying
жр**ёт**	he, she is eating	дохн**ет**	he, she is dying
жр**ём**	we're eating	дохн**ем**	we're dying
жр**ёте**	you're eating	дохн**ете**	you're dying
жр**ут**	they're eating	дохн**ут**	they're dying
жри!	eat!	дохни!	die!
жрал	he was eating	дох	he was dying
жрала	she was eating	дохла	she was dying
жрали	they were eating	дохли	they were dying

There's a world of dirty words — both **мат** and otherwise — remaining to explore in Russian, but at this point, the work of this book is finished. We have looked at all **мат** roots and all the most common expressions formed from them; and, in this final chapter, we've given a sense of the sorts of words that exist on the margins of **мат** and are often used with it. Armed with this knowledge, you should be able to make sense of new expressions as you encounter them.

For this purpose, a few pages have been left blank so that you can collect and compile all your favorite **мат** expressions.

(ROOM FOR COMPILING NEW **MAT** EXPRESSIONS!)

(ROOM FOR COMPILING NEW **MAT** EXPRESSIONS!)

(ROOM FOR COMPILING NEW **MAT** EXPRESSIONS!)

(ROOM FOR COMPILING NEW **MAT** EXPRESSIONS!)

(ROOM FOR COMPILING NEW **MAT** EXPRESSIONS!)

(ROOM FOR COMPILING NEW **MAT** EXPRESSIONS!)

Guide to Verb Types

* asterisks mark a position where a mutation occurs, whenever possible

type	stem	non-past forms	infinitive	past forms
		suffixed stems (both и and ё endings)		
consonant stems + ё endings (-у/-ю, -ёшь, -ёт, -ём, -ёте, -ут/-ют)				
АЙ	чит-ай-	читаю, читаешь... читают	читать: read	читал, читала, читало, читали
ЕЙ	ум-ей-	умею, умеешь... умеют	уметь: know how	умел, умела, умело, умели
	стар-ей-	старею, стареешь... стареют	стареть: grow old	старел, старела, старело, старели
АВАЙ (only 3 basic verbs)	дай-	даю, даёшь... дают (авай → а)	давать: give	давал, давала, давало, давали
	у-знай-	узнаю, узнаёшь... узнают (авай → а)	узнавать: find out	узнавал, узнавала, узнавало, узнавали
	в-стай-	встаю, встаёшь... встают (авай → а)	вставать: get up	вставал, вставала, вставало, вставали
vowel stems + и endings (-у/-ю, -ишь, -ит, -им, -ите, -ат/-ят)				
И (mutation in я form, when possible)	ответ-и-	отвечу*, ответишь... ответят	ответить: answer	ответил, ответила, ответили
	реш-и-	решу, решишь... решат	решить: solve	решил, решила, решили
	люб-и-	люблю*, любишь... любят	любить: love	любил, любила, любило, любили
	говор-и-	говорю, говоришь... говорят	говорить: say, speak	говорил, говорила, звонили
Е (like И)	сид-е-	сижу, сидишь... сидят	сидеть: sit	сидел, сидела, сидело, сидели
	смотр-е-	смотрю, смотришь... смотрят	смотреть: watch	смотрел, смотрела, смотрели
ЖА (ЙА)	леж-а-	лежу, лежишь... лежат	лежать: lie	лежал, лежала, лежало, лежали
	стой-а-	стою, стоишь... стоят	стоять: stand	стоял, стояла, стояло, стояли
vowel stems + ё endings (-у/-ю, -ёшь, -ёт, -ём, -ёте, -ут/-ют)				
А	пис-а-	пишу*, пишешь*... пишут*	писать: write	писал, писала, писало, писали
	смей-а-	смеюсь, смеёшься... смеются	смеяться: laugh	смеялся, смеялась, смеялось, смеялись

type	stem	non-past forms	infinitive	past forms
n/sA	ж/д-а-	жду, ждёшь... ждут	ждать: wait	ждал, ждала, ждало, ждали
	з/в-а-	зову, зовёшь... зовут (inserted о)	звать: call, summon	звал, звала, звало, звали
	б/р-а-	беру, берёшь... берут (inserted е)	брать: take	брал, брала, брало, брали
OBA (EBA)	рис-ова-	рисую, рисуешь... рисуют (ова → у)	рисовать: draw	рисовал, рисовала, рисовали
	танц-ева-	танцую, танцуешь... танцуют (ева → у)	танцевать: dance	танцевал, танцевала, танцевали
	с-ова-	сую, суёшь... суют (ова → у)	совать: stick, shove	совал, совала, совало, совали
	во-ева-	воюю, воюешь... воюют (ева → ю)	воевать: wage war	воевал, воевала, воевало, воевали
O	бор-о-	борюсь, борешься... борются	бороться: struggle	боролся, боролась, боролось, боролись
НУ	отдох-ну-	отдохну, отдохнёшь... отдохнут	отдохнуть: relax	отдохнул, отдохнула, отдохнула, отдохнули
(НУ)	при-вык-ну-	привыкну, привыкнешь... привыкнут	привыкнуть: get used	привык, привыкла, привыкли

non-suffixed stems (ё endings only!)

type	stem	non-past forms	infinitive	past forms
syllabic resonant stems				
В	жив-	живу, живёшь... живут	жить: live	жил, жила, жило, жили
Н	о-ден-	одену, оденешь... оденут	одеть: dress	одел, одела, одело, одели
Й	дуй-	дую, дуешь... дуют	дуть: blow	дул, дула, дуло, дули
ОЙ	мой-	мою, моешь... моют	мыть: wash	мыл, мыла, мыло, мыли
Ь	пь-	пью, пьёшь... пьют	пить: drink	пил, пила, пило, пили
non-syllabic resonant stems				
/Р	ум/р-	умру, умрёшь... умрут	умереть: die	умер, умерла, умерло, умерли
/М	ж/м-	жму, жмёшь... жмут	жать: squeeze	жал, жала, жало, жали
/Н	нач/н-	начну, начнёшь... начнут	начать: begin	начал, начала, начало, начали
Й/М	по-й/м-	пойму, поймёшь... поймут	понять: understand	понял, поняла, поняло, поняли
НИМ	с-ним-	сниму, снимешь... снимут	снять: take off	снял, сняла, сняло, сняли

obstruent stems (note past tense forms and infinitives in -сти / -чь)

Д	вед-	веду, ведёшь... ведут	вести: lead	вёл, вела, вело, вели
Т	мет-	мету, метёшь... метут	мести: sweep	мёл, мела, мело, мели
З	нес-	несу, несёшь... несут	нести: carry	нёс, несла, несло, несли
С	вез-	везу, везёшь... везут	везти: convey	вёз, везла, везло, везли
Г	мог-	могу, можешь*... могут (note г → ж)	мочь: be able	мог, могла, могло, могли
К	пек-	пеку, печёшь*... пекут (note к → ч)	печь: bake	пёк, пекла, пекло, пекли
Б	греб-	гребу, гребёшь... гребут	грести: rake, row	грёб, гребла, гребло, гребли

* asterisks mark a position where a mutation occurs, whenever possible

Guide to All Verbs of Motion

	unprefixed verbs of motion			base pairs for prefixation	
	two imperfective infinitives!		perfective	imperfective	perfective
	indeterminate	determinate	setting out /		
	around / round trip ⟳	underway ↑	assumed arrival ↑		
to go by foot	ходить И	идти (иду, идёшь | шёл, шла, шли)	пойти	-ходить И	-йти
to go by vehicle	ездить И	ехать (еду, едешь, едят)	поехать	-езжать АЙ	-ехать
to go by air, fly	летать АЙ	лететь Е (лечу, летишь)	полететь Е	-летать АЙ	-лететь Е
to run	бегать АЙ	бежать (бегу, бежишь, бегут)	побежать	-бегать АЙ	-бежать
to go by water	плавать АЙ	плыть В (плыву, плывёшь)	поплыть В	-плывать АЙ	-плыть В

basic verbs of conveyance:

to carry (on foot)	носить И	нести С (несу, несёшь | нёс, несла)	понести С	-носить И	-нести С
to lead	водить И	вести Д (веду, ведёшь | вёл, вела)	повести Д	-водить И	-вести Д
to take by vehicle	возить И	везти З (везу, везёшь | вёз, везла)	повезти З	-возить И	-везти З

advanced verbs of motion & conveyance:

to pull, drag	таскать АЙ	тащить Иshift	потащить И	-таскивать АЙ	-тащить И
to drive, chase	гонять АЙ	гнать (гоню, гонишь, гонят)	погнать	-гонять АЙ	-гнать
to climb	лазить И	лезть З (лезу, лезешь | лез, лезла)	полезть З	-лезать АЙ	-лезть З
to crawl, creep	ползать АЙ	ползти З (ползу, ползёшь | полз, -зла)	поползти З	-ползать АЙ	-ползти З
to make roll	катать АЙ	катить Иshift	покатить И	-катывать АЙ	-катить И
to be rolling	кататься АЙ	катиться Иshift	покатиться И	-катываться АЙ	-катиться И
to make tumble	валять АЙ	валить Иshift	повалить И	-валивать АЙ	-валить И
to be tumbling	валяться АЙ	валиться Иshift	повалиться И	-валиваться АЙ	-валиться И
to roam, ramble	бродить Иend	брести Д (бреду, бредёшь | брёл, -ла)	побрести Д	-бредать АЙ	-брести Д

Guide to noun declensions

masculine nouns

hard

	singular	plural
nom.	стол	столы
gen.	стола	столов
acc.	стол	столы
animate:	студента	студентов
dat.	столу	столам
prep.	столе	столах
instr.	столом	столами

soft

	singular	plural	singular	plural
nom.	словарь	словари	музей	музеи
gen.	словаря	словарей	музея	музеев
acc.	словарь	словари	музей	музеи
animate:	писателя	писателей		
dat.	словарю	словарям	музею	музеям
prep.	словаре	словарях	музее	музеях
instr.	словарём	словарями	музеем	музеями

special soft

	singular	plural	singular	plural
nom.	критерий	критерии	гений	гении
gen.	критерия	критериев		
acc.	критерий	критерии		
animate:			гения	гениев
dat.	критерию	критериям		
prep.	**критерии**	критериях		
instr.	критерием	критериями		

feminine nouns

hard

	singular	plural
nom.	газета	газеты
gen.	газеты	газет
acc.	газету	газеты
dat.	газете	газетам
prep.	газете	газетах
instr.	газетой	газетами

soft

	singular	plural
nom.	неделя	недели
gen.	недели	недель
acc.	неделю	недели
dat.	неделе	неделям
prep.	неделе	неделях
instr.	неделей	неделями
instr.	семьёй	семьями

special soft

	singular	plural
nom.	**лекция**	лекции
gen.	лекции	лекций
acc.	лекцию	лекции
dat.	лекции	лекциям
prep.	**лекции**	лекциях
instr.	лекцией	лекциями

и-nouns

	singular	plural
nom.	тетрадь	тетради
gen.	тетради	тетрадей
acc.	тетрадь	тетради
dat.	тетради	тетрадям
prep.	тетради	тетрадях
instr.	тетрадью	тетрадями

neuter nouns

hard

soft

special soft

окно

	singular	plural
nom.	окно	окна
gen.	окна	окон
acc.	окно	окна
dat.	окну	окнам
prep.	окне	окнах
instr.	окном	окнами

friend

	друг (sg.)	друг (pl.)
nom.	друг	друзья
gen.	друга	друзей
acc.	друга	друзей
dat.	другу	друзьям
prep.	друге	друзьях
instr.	другом	друзьями

master, host, landlord

	хозяин (sg.)	хозяин (pl.)
nom.	хозяин	хозяева
gen.	хозяина	хозяев
acc.	хозяина	хозяев
dat.	хозяину	хозяевам
prep.	хозяине	хозяевах
instr.	хозяином	хозяевами

море / бельё

	singular море	singular бельё	plural моря	plural
nom.	море	бельё	моря	—
gen.	моря	белья	морей	—
acc.	море	бельё	моря	—
dat.	морю	белью	морям	—
prep.	море	белье	морях	—
instr.	морем	бельём	морями	—

son

	сын (sg.)	сын (pl.)
nom.	сын	сыновья
gen.	сына	сыновей
acc.	сына	сыновей
dat.	сыну	сыновьям
prep.	сыне	сыновьях
instr.	сыном	сыновьями

brother

	брат (sg.)	брат (pl.)
nom.	брат	братья
gen.	брата	братьев
acc.	брата	братьев
dat.	брату	братьям
prep.	брате	братьях
instr.	братом	братьями

здание

	singular	plural
nom.	здание	здания
gen.	здания	зданий
acc.	здание	здания
dat.	зданию	зданиям
prep.	здании	зданиях
instr.	зданием	зданиями

sister

	сестра (sg.)	сестра (pl.)
nom.	сестра	сёстры
gen.	сестры	сестёр
acc.	сестру	сестёр
dat.	сестре	сёстрам
prep.	сестре	сёстрах
instr.	сестрой	сёстрами

neighbor

	сосед (sg.)	сосед (pl.)
nom.	сосед	соседи
gen.	соседа	соседей
acc.	соседа	соседей
dat.	соседу	соседям
prep.	соседе	соседях
instr.	соседом	соседями

child

	ребёнок (sg.)	ребёнок (pl.)
nom.	ребёнок	дети
gen.	ребёнка	детей
acc.	ребёнка	детей
dat.	ребёнку	детям
prep.	ребёнке	детях
instr.	ребёнком	детьми

daughter

	дочь (sg.)	дочь (pl.)
nom.	дочь	дочери
gen.	дочери	дочерей
acc.	дочь	дочерей
dat.	дочери	дочерям
prep.	дочери	дочерях
instr.	дочерью	дочерями

mother

	мать (sg.)	мать (pl.)
nom.	мать	матери
gen.	матери	матерей
acc.	мать	матерей
dat.	матери	матерям
prep.	матери	матерях
instr.	матерью	матерями

person, human being

	человек (sg.)	человек (pl.)
nom.	человек	люди
gen.	человека	людей
acc.	человека	людей
dat.	человеку	людям
prep.	человеке	людях
instr.	человеком	людьми

Guide to declension of names

female names

	имя	отчество	фамилия
nom.	Марина	Ивановна	Цветаева
gen.	Марины	Ивановны	Цветаевой
acc.	Марину	Ивановну	Цветаеву
dat.	Марине	Ивановне	Цветаевой
prep.	Марине	Ивановне	Цветаевой
instr.	Мариной	Ивановной	Цветаевой

male names

	имя	отчество	фамилия
nom.	Михаил	Афанасьевич	Булгаков
gen.	Михаила	Афанасьевича	Булгакова
acc.	Михаила	Афанасьевича	Булгакова
dat.	Михаилу	Афанасьевичу	Булгакову
prep.	Михаиле	Афанасьевиче	Булгакове
instr.	Михаилом	Афанасьевичем	Булгаковым

short forms

	Михаил	Дарья
nom.	Миша	Даша
gen.	Миши	Даши
acc.	Мишу	Дашу
dat.	Мише	Даше
prep.	Мише	Даше
instr.	Мишей	Дашей

	male	female
nom.	Маяковский	Маяковская
gen.	Маяковского	Маяковской
acc.	Маяковского	Маяковскую
dat.	Маяковскому	Маяковской
prep.	Маяковском	Маяковской
instr.	Маяковским	Маяковской

	male	female
nom.	Бахтин	Бахтина
gen.	Бахтина	Бахтиной
acc.	Бахтина	Бахтину
dat.	Бахтину	Бахтиной
prep.	Бахтине	Бахтиной
instr.	Бахтиным	Бахтиной

Пастернак	Барак Обама
Пастернака	Барака Обамы
Пастернака	Барака Обаму
Пастернаку	Бараку Обаме
Пастернаке	Бараке Обаме
Пастернаком	Бараком Обамой

Guide to declension of pronouns

	what?	who?	I	you (s.)	we	you (pl.)	he (masc.)	she (fem.)	it (neut.)	they
nom.	что	кто	я	ты	мы	вы	он	она	оно	они
gen.	чего	кого	меня	тебя	нас	вас	его него	её неё	его него	их них
acc.	что	кого	меня	тебя	нас	вас	его него	её неё	его него	их них
dat.	чему	кому	мне	тебе	нам	вам	ему нему	ей ней	ему нему	им ним
prep.	чём	ком	мне	тебе	нас	вас	— нём	— ней	— нём	— них
instr.	чем	кем	мной	тобой	нами	вами	им ним	ей ней	им ним	ими ними

	oneself
nom.	—
gen.	себя
acc.	себя
dat.	себе
prep.	себе
instr.	собой

	each other		
acc.	друг друга	Мы хорошо знаем друг друга.	each other
dat.	друг другу	Мы всегда помогаем друг другу.	each other

A preposition typically falls in the middle, and, again, only the second **друг** declines:

acc.	друг на друга	Они смотрели друг на друга.	at each other
gen.	друг без друга	Мы не можем жить друг без друга.	without each other
dat.	друг к другу	Мы привыкли друг к другу.	to each other
prep.	друг о друге	Они часто думают друг о друге.	about each other
instr.	друг с другом	Мы ходили в театр друг с другом.	with each other

Guide to declension of adjectives

masculine singular

	special modifiers						hard adjectives	soft adjectives
nom.	этот	весь	один	чей	мой	наш	новый	синий
gen.	этого	всего	одного	чьего	моего	нашего	нового	синего
acc.	этот	весь	один	чей	мой	наш	новый	синий
animate:	этого	всего	одного	чьего	моего	нашего	нового	синего
dat.	этому	всему	одному	чьему	моему	нашему	новому	синему
prep.	этом	всём	одном	чьём	моём	нашем	новом	синем
instr.	этим	всем	одним	чьим	моим	нашим	новым	синим

feminine singular

	special modifiers						hard adjectives	soft adjectives
nom.	эта	вся	одна	чья	моя	наша	новая	синяя
gen.	этой	всей	одной	чьей	моей	нашей	новой	синей
acc.	эту	всю	одну	чью	мою	нашу	новую	синюю
dat.	этой	всей	одной	чьей	моей	нашей	новой	синей
prep.	этой	всей	одной	чьей	моей	нашей	новой	синей
instr.	этой	всей	одной	чьей	моей	нашей	новой	синей

neuter singular

	special modifiers						hard adjectives	soft adjectives
nom.	это	всё	одно	чьё	моё	наше	новое	синее
gen.	этого	всего	одного	чьего	моего	нашего	нового	синего
acc.	это	всё	одно	чьё	моё	наше	новое	синее
dat.	этому	всему	одному	чьему	моему	нашему	новому	синему
prep.	этом	всём	одном	чьём	моём	нашем	новом	синем
instr.	этим	всем	одним	чьим	моим	нашим	новым	синим

plural (for all three genders)

	special modifiers						hard adjectives	soft adjectives
nom.	эти	все	одни	чьи	мои	наши	новые	синие
gen.	этих	всех	одних	чьих	моих	наших	новых	синих
acc.	эти	все	одни	чьи	мои	наши	новые	синие
animate:	этих	всех	одних	чьих	моих	наших	новых	синих
dat.	этим	всем	одним	чьим	моим	нашим	новым	синим
prep.	этих	всех	одних	чьих	моих	наших	новых	синих
instr.	этими	всеми	одними	чьими	моими	нашими	новыми	синими

Guide to declension of possessive pronouns

мой / твой / свой

all decline according to this pattern.

	masculine		feminine		neuter	
nom.	мой	торт	моя	бутылка	моё	мыло
gen.	моего	торта	моей	бутылки	моего	мыла
acc.	мой	торт	мою	бутылку	моё	мыло
anim.	моего	друга				
dat.	моему	торту	моей	бутылке	моему	мылу
prep.	моём	торте	моей	бутылке	моём	мыле
instr.	моим	тортом	моей	бутылкой	моим	мылом

наш / ваш

both decline according to this pattern.

	masculine		feminine		neuter	
nom.	наш	торт	наша	бутылка	наше	мыло
gen.	нашего	торта	нашей	бутылки	нашего	мыла
acc.	наш	торт	нашу	бутылку	наше	мыло
anim.	нашего	друга				
dat.	нашему	торту	нашей	бутылке	нашему	мылу
prep.	нашем	торте	нашей	бутылке	нашем	мыле
instr.	нашим	тортом	нашей	бутылкой	нашим	мылом

Other special modifiers

	masculine		feminine		neuter	
nom.	весь	торт	вся	бутылка	всё	мыло
gen.	всего	торта	всей	бутылки	всего	мыла
acc.	весь	торт	всю	бутылку	всё	мыло
anim.	всего	человека				
dat.	всему	торту	всей	бутылке	всему	мылу
prep.	всём	торте	всей	бутылке	всём	мыле
instr.	всем	тортом	всей	бутылкой	всем	мылом

	masc.	fem.	neut.
nom.	один	одна	одно
gen.	одного	одной	одного
acc.	один	одну	одно
anim.	одного		
dat.	одному	одной	одному
prep.	одном	одной	одном
instr.	одним	одной	одним

	masc.	fem.	neut.
nom.	чей	чья	чьё
gen.	чьего	чьей	чьего
acc.	чей	чью	чьё
anim.	чьего		
dat.	чьему	чьей	чьему
prep.	чьём	чьей	чьём
instr.	чьим	чьей	чьим

Numbers (cardinal and ordinal)

singles
use **две** with fem.*

1	**один**
2	**два** (две)
3	**три**
4	**четыре**
5	**пять**
6	**шесть**
7	**семь**
8	**восемь**
9	**девять**
10	**десять**

teens
note the lost ь's in front of -**надцать**

11	**одиннадцать**
12	**двенадцать**
13	**тринадцать**
14	**четырнадцать**
15	**пятнадцать**
16	**шестнадцать**
17	**семнадцать**
18	**восемнадцать**
19	**девятнадцать**

tens
but, the ь remains in front of -**десят**:

10	**десять**
20	**двадцать**
30	**тридцать**
40	**сорок**
50	**пятьдесят**
60	**шестьдесят**
70	**семьдесят**
80	**восемьдесят**
90	**девяносто**

compound
just combine tens and singles, with **no hypen**

21	**двадцать один**
22	**двадцать два**
23	**двадцать три**
24	**двадцать четыре**
25	**двадцать пять**
26	**двадцать шесть**
27	**двадцать семь**
28	**двадцать восемь**
29	**двадцать девять**

hundreds
keep the ь before -**сот**

100	**сто**
200	**двести**
300	**триста**
400	**четыреста**
500	**пятьсот**
600	**шестьсот**
700	**семьсот**
800	**восемьсот**
900	**девятьсот**

thousands
2, 3, 4 take **тысячи**, 5 take **тысяч**

1,000	**тысяча**
2,000	две **тысячи**
3,000	три **тысячи**
4,000	четыре **тысячи**
5,000	пять **тысяч**
6,000	шесть **тысяч**
7,000	семь **тысяч**
8,000	восемь **тысяч**
9,000	девять **тысяч**
10,000	десять **тысяч**

singles

один	1st	**первый**
два (две)	2nd	**второй**
три	3rd	**Третий**
четыре	4th	**четвёртый**
пять	5th	**пятый**
шесть	6th	**шестой**
семь	7th	**седьмой**
восемь	8th	**восьмой**
девять	9th	**девятый**
десять	10th	**десятый**

teens

11th	**одиннадцатый**
12th	**двенадцатый**
13th	**тринадцатый**
14th	**четырнадцатый**
15th	**пятнадцатый**
16th	**шестнадцатый**
17th	**семнадцатый**
18th	**восемнадцатый**
19th	**девятнадцатый**

tens and one hundred

десять	10th	**десятый**
двадцать	20th	**двадцатый**
тридцать	30th	**тридцатый**
сорок	40th	**сороковой**
пятьдесят	50th	**пятидесятый**
шестьдесят	60th	**шестидесятый**
семьдесят	70th	**семидесятый**
восемьдесят	80th	**восьмидесятый**
девяносто	90th	**девяностый**
сто	100th	**сотый**

ordinary soft adjectives

	masc.	fem.	neut.	plural
nom.	синий	синяя	синее	синие
gen.	синего	синей	синего	
acc.	синий	синюю	синее	
animate:	синего			
dat.	синему	синей	синему	
prep.	синем	синей	синем	
instr.	синим	синей	синим	

третий - third

	masc.	fem.	neut.	plural
nom.	третий	третья	третье	третьи
gen.	третьего	третьей	третьего	
acc.	третий	третью	третье	
animate:	третьего			
dat.	третьему	третьей	третьему	
prep.	третьем	третьей	третьем	
instr.	третьим	третьей	третьим	

Common neuter singular short-form adjectives / adverbs

	long-form	short-form / adverb
good	хороший →	хорошо
bad	плохой →	плохо
understood	понятный →	понятно
strange	странный →	странно
clear	ясный →	ясно
hard	трудный →	трудно
heavy	тяжёлый →	тяжело
easy / light	лёгкий →	легко
excellent	отличный →	отлично
sweet, nice	милый →	мило
stupid	глупый →	глупо

	long-form	short-form / adverb
sad	грустный →	грустно
funny	смешной →	смешно
awful	ужасный →	ужасно
terrible, scary	страшный →	страшно
unbelievable	невероятный →	невероятно
obvious	очевидный →	очевидно
curious, odd	любопытный →	любопытно
(un)interesting	(не)интересный →	(не)интересно
(un)pleasant	(не)приятный →	(не)приятно
(in)convenient	(не)удобный →	(не)удобно
(not) pretty, nice	(не)красивый →	(не)красиво

Common short-form adjectives

	long-form	short-form (used in the nominative only)			
certain, sure	уверенный →	уверен	увере́на	увере́но	увере́ны
drunk	пьяный →	пьян	пьяна́	пьяно́	пьяны́
sober	трезвый →	трезв	трезва́	тре́зво	тре́звы
healthy	здоро́вый →	здоро́в	здоро́ва	здоро́во	здоро́вы
ready, finished	гото́вый →	гото́в	гото́ва	гото́во	гото́вы
happy	счастливый →	счастлив	счастлива	счастливо	счастливы
busy, occupied	заня́тый* →	за́нят	занята́	за́нято	за́няты
sated, full	сы́тый →	сыт	сыта́	сы́то	сы́ты
alive	живо́й →	жив	жива́	жи́во	жи́вы
dead	мёртвый →	мёртв	мертва́	мертво́	мертвы́
satisfied	дово́льный →	дово́лен	дово́льна	дово́льно	дово́льны
free, available	свобо́дный →	свобо́ден	свобо́дна	свобо́дно	свобо́дны
hungry	голо́дный →	голо́ден	голодна́	го́лодно	голо́дны
sick, ill	больно́й →	бо́лен	больна́	больно́	больны́
needed, necessary	ну́жный →	ну́жен	нужна́	ну́жно	нужны́
in agreement (+ **c**)*	согла́сный →	согла́сен	согла́сна	согла́сно	согла́сны

Guide to (irregular) comparatives

irregular comparatives

big	большой → больше	bigger, more
small	маленький → меньше	smaller, less
good	хороший → лучше	better
bad	плохой → хуже	worse
far, remote	далёкий → дальше	further
cheap	дешёвый → дешевле	cheaper
late	поздний → позже	later
early	ранний → раньше	earlier
young	молодой → младше	younger*
old	старый → старше	older
long (of time)	долгий → дольше	for a longer time

comparatives involving (regular) mutations

З / Г / Д → Ж

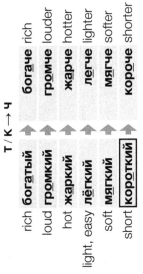

expensive	дорогой → дороже	more exp.
young	молодой → моложе	younger*
hard, firm	твёрдый → твёрже	harder
near, close	близкий → ближе	closer
narrow	узкий → уже	narrower
low, short	низкий → ниже	lower

Т / К → Ч

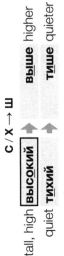

rich	богатый → богаче	rich
loud	громкий → громче	louder
hot	жаркий → жарче	hotter
light, easy	лёгкий → легче	lighter
soft	мягкий → мягче	softer
short	короткий → короче	shorter

С / Х → Ш

tall, high	высокий → выше	higher
quiet	тихий → тише	quieter

СТ → Щ

simple	простой → проще	simpler
frequent	частый → чаще	more often